The Sending Church Applied is ⟨...⟩ to
take seriously its role in missior ⟨...⟩ :al
tips for each of the seventeen S ⟨...⟩ .aff
will be forever indebted to La ⟨...⟩ for
the impact they have had on ou. ⟨...⟩ any
years ago through a series of consultations as we walked ⟨...⟩ ach
of the elements described in this book. Now, this invaluable resource
is available for your church team to walk through together.

As we read through the book, we were struck by areas where we still
need to grow, such as "proactive versus reactive" identification of potential missionaries. We are still learning! And yet so much of the sending
culture at our church traces its roots back to Upstream and the principles
found in *The Sending Church Applied*. Assessment, development, and
advocacy teams are just a few of the concepts now part of the regular
rhythms of Johnson Ferry sending. We thank God for these Upstream
leaders! Due to their tireless efforts, our church has sent more people
to the field than ever before. And as a result, more of the unreached are
hearing and responding to the gospel.

Brian Fox, Chris White, & Nicole Bush | Global Sending Team, Johnson
Ferry Baptist Church, Atlanta, Georgia

Just as missions is moving away from previous colonial attitudes and
toward a healthy collaborative approach with local partners, another
partnership that must be re-examined is that between the missionary
and the local church. Building on the mandates in Scripture and its pre-
decessor, *The Sending Church Defined*, this book follows up with the
actual steps for churches to "take back" what has been delegated to
missions agencies. Describing seventeen elements for establishment,
development, engagement, and multiplication of a healthy sending
church, the authors have crafted a blueprint for sending well.

Its focus on relationships and reciprocity with the missionary deeply
resonates with me. As someone who has worked overseas in a very
difficult context for many years, I rely heavily on my sending church. *The
Sending Church Applied* offers motivation, encouragement, and actual
frameworks for the relationship between the missionary and the sending
church. It seeks to involve the entire church body, enhance collaboration with agencies, and deepen the reciprocal relationship between the

church and the missionary. I plan to share this book widely—with my agency leaders, as they help our members to expand connections with the church, and with my teammates and other missionaries, as we seek to strengthen the bonds between those who send and the sent ones.

Elizabeth George | medical missionary educator, creative-access country (name changed for security)

"I don't know where to begin...It all seems too complicated...This isn't where my strength lies so let's focus on something else...Let's just do what we've always done to save time and effort..." We all know how tiring and trying it can be to integrate global mission thinking and a 'sent' mentality into the culture and practice of any local church family. Yet what could be more important for the spiritual health and gospel life of a congregation than helping them to love and live out God's glorious global gospel promises to the ends of the earth!

In this wonderful book, Bradley, Mike, Larry, and Nathan, four of the most gifted and passionate authors I've read, lay down seventeen 'building blocks' to help any church respond fervently, faithfully, and fruitfully to God's gracious invitation to join him in his Great Commission purposes both locally and globally. Biblically grounded from start to finish, this book is clear and practical, inspiring and exciting, hopeful and helpful, and will encourage and equip local churches to be who they're called to be—the sent and sending people of God. I hugely enjoyed and benefited from reading this book, and I strongly suspect you will too. Read on!

Chris Howles | Director of Cross Cultural Training, Oak Hill College, London, United Kingdom

THE SENDING CHURCH APPLIED

THE SENDING CHURCH APPLIED

Bradley Bell, Mike Easton,
Larry McCrary, Nathan Sloan

UPSTREAM

Permissions
The Upstream Collective
900 E Jefferson St
Louisville, KY 40206

www.theupstreamcollective.org

ISBN: 979-8-9901754-1-9

Printed in the United States of America

Editors: David McWhite and Meredith Cook
Cover and interior design: Hayley Moss, Moss Photo and Design, LLC
hayleyrmoss@gmail.com

For the churches where we observed the Sending Church Elements
For the churches who will use them
For the churches who will make them better

ABOUT THE AUTHORS

Bradley Bell, Executive Director of Upstream Equipping

Bradley leads Upstream Equipping, a ministry of the Upstream Collective, focused on equipping churches to send well. He has over twenty years of experience as a missionary, missions pastor, lead pastor, and missiologist. He is also the author of multiple Upstream books, including *The Sending Church Defined* and *Lent and Missions: A 40-Day Devotional*. Bradley writes for numerous publications, which are compiled at beautifulmissiology.com. He is married to Katie, and they have four daughters, all named after missionaries; Elisabeth, Charlotte, Anneliese, and Madeleine. They live in Louisville, Kentucky.

Mike Easton, Director of Content for Upstream Collective; Reliant International Program Manager

Mike spent eight years as the missions pastor at Cornerstone Church in Ames, Iowa. Before that Mike and his wife, Emily, served for two years in East Asia with the International Mission Board and returned with a vision to send people to the nations. In his role as missions pastor, Mike was able to see many mobilized into missions, play a role in the formation of overseas teams, and pass on practical lessons learned as a missions leader to other churches.

Larry McCrary, Co-Founder and President of Upstream Collective

Larry and his family have lived in Europe for nearly twenty years, where he has served in a variety of strategy and leadership roles. Prior to moving to Europe, he was a church planter and pastor in the United States. He is a co-author of *Tradecraft: For the Church on Mission*, *The First 30 Daze: Practical Encouragement for Living Abroad Intentionally*, and *The MarketSpace: Essential Relationships Between the Sending Church, Marketplace Worker, and Missionary Team*.

Nathan Sloan, Executive Director of Upstream Sending

Nathan leads Upstream Sending, a ministry of the Upstream Collective, focused on church-centric global sending. His work focuses on helping churches and church leaders send well. He is the author of *You Are Sent: Finding Your Place in God's Global Mission* and *Multisite Missions Leadership*, and the co-author of *Lent and Missions: A 40-Day Devotional*. Previously, Nathan was the missions pastor at Sojourn Church Midtown in Louisville, Kentucky, and before that served with his wife, Sarah, as a missionary in Nepal. Nathan has a doctorate in missiology from the Southern Baptist Theological Seminary.

TABLE OF CONTENTS

FOREWORD

In my undergraduate days I majored in natural sciences. When God called me into pastoral and church planting ministry, he also called me to change my educational focus. Instead of studying mitochondria, I studied missiology. I moved from discoveries in chemistry to discovering ways to plant churches effectively. Despite the shift in the focus of my life's work, I've always retained an interest in the natural sciences. I've especially appreciated the way that these sciences illuminate our wonder at the amazing world God created and, ultimately, our worship of God himself. What's more, I've found that the natural sciences provide another way to talk about the truth of God (theology) and the mission of God (missiology).

For example, you might remember from high school chemistry that the periodic table organizes the known elements of the created world. The elements relate to one another in various ways based on their placement in the same column (or "group") and row (or "period"). This table can also provide insight for the mission of God through the church, as Bradley Bell, Mike Easton, Larry McCrary, and Nathan Sloan show us in *The Sending Church Applied*. These authors in this way help leaders break down various critical components related to missions and sending from the local church, guiding readers through seventeen "Sending Church Elements."

The analogy of the periodic table helps *The Sending Church Applied* accomplish exactly what its name says: the book applies God's Word and God's call with clarity and precision. It outlines the varying and complex elements of the church's task of global mission in a coherent and practical way. In doing this, the book makes such complexities more orderly and doable. The authors bring a wealth of experience into their writing, as combined they have served in a variety of ministry and missional settings. Leveraging this, they highlight and illustrate the seventeen Sending Church

Elements across four phases, from Establishing to Developing, Engaging, and Multiplying.

Now, if science doesn't thrill you like it thrills me, don't worry. Don't let the scientific metaphor fool you into thinking that this book is dry like a middle school textbook. Instead, to use a different metaphor, think of *The Sending Church Applied* as a feast for those who hunger for God's purpose, God's mission, and, ultimately, God's glory. Rather than a fast-food combo of ministry hacks, the following pages will nourish you with rich, savory, and nutritious wisdom. Any church serious about becoming a sending church should start here.

Ed Stetzer
Dean, Talbot School of Theology

INTRODUCTION

One of the most pivotal experiences of a student's life is their introduction to the periodic table. For the scientifically minded, this is a happy memory. For others of us, we're already bored again at the thought of it. Regardless of our response, the table represented a doorway to the world of chemistry. The little blocks with numbers and letters revealed a complex world of elements. Studying it made us see that the universe's biggest things are made up of the universe's smallest things. You can start with atoms and end up with galaxies. Mind blowing!

This book is a periodic table of global missions for the local church. It reveals seventeen "elements" that make up what we call a "sending church." After years of working within and alongside local churches, we at Upstream Collective discovered a lack of clarity about how to engage in God's global mission. Some believed it was simply a matter of sending money. Others found it sufficient for missions organizations to carry out the work. And yet the Scriptures cast a vision for so much more. The sending church needed definition.

The Sending Church Defined

We were determined to get answers and to get them from practitioners. So we gathered a group of sending church leaders, put them in a room with a white board and lots of coffee, and asked them to define a sending church. They labored over every word and arrived at the following definition:

> A sending church is a local community of Christ-followers who have made a covenant together to be prayerful, deliberate, and proactive in developing, commissioning, and sending their own members both locally and globally, often in partnership

with other churches or agencies, and continuing to encourage, support, and advocate for them while making disciples cross-culturally and upon their return.

Yes, we understand this reads like one of the apostle Paul's run-on sentences. But we wanted to be specific. It needed to be clear that faithful missions engagement was not simply a matter of sending money or prayers but also of sending *people*. Our conviction was that all Christians are "sent ones" on mission in their everyday lives, and some of them are sent as missionaries.

We then took the definition and wrote an essay for every word. That's right, we defined a definition! The result became a foundational book for Upstream. It was called *The Sending Church Defined*. Think of it as introducing the *theory* of a sending church. We've found that it resonates with missions leaders all over the world.

Yet, because these leaders are practitioners, we've also found that theory isn't enough. They want application. They want to know, How does a sending church *work*?

The Sending Church Elements

At this point, Upstream leaders took on the task of closely studying sending churches of different sizes and contexts that we have developed relationships with over the years—not simply studying best practices but also these congregations' overarching stories. We asked how they became sending churches. They clearly believed in the centrality of the local church in God's global mission, but how did they put that belief into action?

From this study, we began to recognize some patterns. We call these patterns "elements"—practical building blocks for sending well. Eventually, we identified seventeen of them. Although the elements are more cyclical than linear, we found we could categorize them into different "phases" of sending church maturity. These phases are:

» **Establishing**: The church lays a biblical foundation for sending.
» **Developing**: The church prepares its own members to be sent.
» **Engaging**: The church sends and sustains its own members.
» **Multiplying**: The church matures in its sending ability and influence.

When we ordered the seventeen elements according to the four phases, something looked familiar. There it was again—the periodic table! For the full color version, see the back cover.

ESTABLISHING	DEVELOPING	ENGAGING	MULTIPLYING
01 **Cu** CULTIVATING MISSIONS AWARENESS	06 **Ev** EVALUATING SENDING PATHWAYS AND PARTNERS	10 **Co** COMMISSIONING MISSIONARIES	14 **Iv** INVITING MISSIONARIES' INFLUENCE
02 **Es** ESTABLISHING MISSIONS CONVICTIONS	07 **Id** IDENTIFYING MISSIONARIES	11 **Ge** GETTING MISSIONARIES ESTABLISHED	15 **Re** RECEIVING MISSIONARIES DURING REENTRY
03 **De** DEVELOPING A VISION	08 **As** ASSESSING MISSIONARIES	12 **Pr** PROVIDING ONGOING CARE	16 **Is** INNOVATING AS SENDING CHURCHES
04 **Bu** BUILDING A STRATEGY	09 **Dm** DEVELOPING MISSIONARIES	13 **Ma** MAINTAINING STRATEGIC FOCUS	17 **Ic** INFLUENCING OTHER CHURCHES
05 **In** INVOLVING THE ENTIRE CHURCH			

This table represents way more than theory. It has taken a complex world of sending church principles and distilled them into actionable steps. These are the small, local things that eventually lead to big, global things. Pair them with a congregation's abiding relationship with Jesus, and both the church and the nations will be changed. We're seeing it happen all over the world.

The Sending Church Applied

The elements above are what we at Upstream use as the centerpiece for all our training, consulting, cohorts, and content. It's often how we'll begin a conversation with a church leader or missionary: "Read over these elements and evaluate your church." We find that many churches are still in the first phase. Others may be further in their sending journey but missing key elements along the way. All of them are excited to have concrete guidance.

From these interactions, we then developed extensive content on each element (you can visit theupstreamcollective.org/resources to see some of it; or for access to all past and future content, you can become a member at theupstreamcollective.org/join). Yet considering the global church's growing desire to send well, we determined that individual resources were not enough. In order to come alongside churches from Guatemala to Spain to Malawi, the content needed to be compiled in one place and accessible in all places. It was time for a second volume: *The Sending Church Applied*.

The book you now hold is organized in the most straightforward way possible: there are seventeen chapters, each devoted to one element. Every chapter defines and explains its element, then it provides actionable steps. You may choose to read through the book chronologically in order to grasp the big picture. This could be a helpful path for the church that's starting from scratch (or undoing some missions malpractice). You might also go directly to the chapters that are most relevant to your church's stage in sending. If you have a missions leadership team, we encourage you to read it together. And for a deeper dive, consider joining one of our Sending Church Elements cohorts (theupstreamcollective.org/cohorts).

The Sending Church Applied was intentionally written by a team of Upstream leaders: Larry McCrary, Nathan Sloan, Mike Easton, and Bradley Bell. These authors are themselves veteran practitioners, each having served in the contexts of cross-cultural missions, the local church, and missions organizations. Since they were assigned specific chapters based on their areas of expertise, the individual author is listed at the beginning of each chapter. It may be helpful to know, however, that the entire process was collaborative. The voices may vary, but the conviction does not.

Furthermore, we consider this book—like all that we produce—to originate ultimately in the sending God and his sending church. Were it not for God sharing himself with us through the gospel, we would not exist. And were it not for churches sharing their struggles and successes with us, this book would not exist. We are grateful!

The Sending Church Language

Just as language matters to the work of making disciples cross-culturally, we recognize that well-defined terms matter in books like this. Though we decided against providing an exhaustive glossary of terms, we do want to clarify our intentional usage of certain words and ideas. For example, we have summarized our overarching approach to missions under the term "sending church" (see earlier in the Introduction for its full definition). Can other words be used to describe this paradigm (such as "church-based missions")? Absolutely. We have simply chosen a single term in order to communicate clearly.

Another important phrase you will encounter in these pages is "sent one(s)." By "sent one(s)" we are referring to *all* Christians, not simply vocational missionaries or Christians living missional lifestyles. What we are communicating here draws directly from our theological conviction that God is a "sending God"—from the union and communion of the Triune God, he moves outwardly in love with a mission to form a global people who are loved by the Father, redeemed by the Son, and sanctified by the Holy Spirit.

Since God is by nature a sending God, all Christians are also by nature his little sent ones—given a place in his global mission when they enter into Christ. We understand that other terms can be used to describe this, and that sometimes people (including us!) have used "sent one(s)" to refer to vocational missionaries. But within these pages, "sent one(s)" consistently refers to all Christians.

Finally, we come to the much-debated word "missionary." Though it arguably can be used in multiple ways, we landed on a singular meaning in this book: a "missionary" is a person who has been sent across linguistic and cultural boundaries to contribute to the mission of making disciples of all nations.

Yes, this usage does defer to vocational missionaries rather than everyday Christians, but we also use it in reference to less traditional Christian workers, such as marketplace professionals, students, intentional travelers, short-termers, mid-termers, medical professionals, educators, retirees, humanitarian workers—anyone whom the church views as sent cross-culturally to contribute to the mission of making disciples of all nations. Of course, readers are welcome to use "missionary" differently in their respective contexts and may be wise to do so for the sake of security. This is only our choice for the sake of continuity in this book.

The Sending Church Blessing

Now, as you embark on the journey ahead, we want to share with you a blessing for the road. Know that as you commit to exploring the elements that make up the sending church, we have prayed for you. You and your church may feel insignificant in the galaxy of global missions, but thanks be to our sending God, you are not insignificant. You are something else—you are *sent*.

Receive this word of assurance drawn from the Scriptures:

Just as the Father sent the Son, (Galatians 4:4)
And the Father and Son sent the Spirit, (John 15:26)
And the Father, Son, and Spirit sent the church, (Acts 1:8)
May you who have been immersed in the Triune God (Matt. 28:19)
Hear him speaking, "Even so, I am sending you," (John 20:21)
And so respond, "Here am I, send me!" (Isaiah 6:8)
For the sake of his glory, (Habakkuk 2:14)
For the sake of the nations, (Psalm 67:2)
And for the sake of your joy. (John 15:11)
This is who he created you to be: (Genesis 1:28)
You are sent.

Amen.

PART 1: ESTABLISHING PHASE

The church lays a biblical foundation for sending.

In the "Establishing" phase of the Sending Church Elements you will seek to lay a biblical foundation for sending that is practically and uniquely applied in your church. Elements #1 and #2 focus on helping church members become aware of God's heart for the nations and then determining your missions convictions. Elements #3, #4, and #5 will take those biblical convictions and use them as the foundation for developing a vision and strategy that will involve the entire church body.

01

Cu

CULTIVATING
MISSIONS
AWARENESS

SENDING CHURCH ELEMENT #1: CULTIVATING MISSIONS AWARENESS

By Bradley Bell

"

A sending church cultivates missions awareness by instilling a holistic culture of God's mission rather than simply a missions ministry. Instead of beginning with activity, the church fosters a sent identity, a missional lens through which to see all of life. Church leaders first give attention to growth in their own missiology, then help their fellow leaders and members to know the local and global calling that flows from God's heart.

Go watch a baby eat cake. No really, if you want to get the basics of this chapter, go watch a baby eat cake. Of course, it has to be according to tradition. The child cannot have eaten cake until her first birthday. It must be laid before her as a mystery. Will it be love at first bite? Will it become just a gooey toy? I am told that I somehow managed to sit on mine.

No matter what happens, the point is that you will get to watch raw cuteness as taste buds and tummy encounter concentrated sugar. You'll see this child awaken to the sucrose molecules that will woo her forever. This discovery for her will be a delight for you. How fun! And how *profound*.

A Whole New World

One of the great delights of being a leader in the local church is seeing people discover the purpose for which God created them. Whether it's a new Christian still in disbelief about the goodness of the gospel, or an aged believer experiencing discipleship for the first time, introducing them to the mission of God is a fun and profound opportunity. That's probably part of why you're reading this book.

It might also be why you would expect us to begin with the Great Commission in Matthew 28:18–20. That is, after all, the most popular passage for relating to global missions. However, cultivating missions awareness in a local church is most effective when it stands upon a foundation. A baby doesn't eat cake on her first day home from the hospital. Her mouth and stomach must be given time to develop. In the same way, a sending church gives time to develop a holistic culture of God's mission.

But what does that mean?

Culture before Ministry

When a local church forgoes what we call a "sending culture" and begins at the point of building a missions ministry, the impact is almost always limited. This is because, according to the structure of many churches, ministries are naturally in competition for things like budget, staffing, communication—as well as participants! If missions is simply a ministry alongside other ministries, then it will inevitably involve only a limited number of church members. You may appeal to the entire church for missions giving campaigns, prayer initiatives, and short-term mission trips, but only *some* will choose to participate. "No thanks," people say. "Missions really isn't my thing."

A sending culture, on the other hand, helps Christians to see that the *entire* purpose of the church is wrapped up in God's redemptive mission. One way to think of it is like putting on glasses. Glasses literally become the lenses through which you see the world. When God's mission becomes the lens through which a local church sees the world, suddenly you have far more than a ministry. Instead, you have a culture that informs every ministry and involves every member (more on this in Chapter 5, "Involving the Entire Church").

For this reason we encourage you to begin far earlier than the Great Commission. A great sending church begins with a great sending God, therefore cultivating missions awareness doesn't even start at Genesis 1. It starts in eternity past.

Identity before Activity

Who is God? He is one God in three Persons, which means within the union of the Godhead there is also communion. There is the expression and reception of unified love, as Jesus alludes to in John 17:24: "Father, I desire that they also, whom you have given me, may be with me where I am, to see my glory that you have given me because *you loved me before the foundation of the world*" (emphasis mine).

It is no wonder, then, that God lovingly sent his word outside himself to create the world and initiate a mission. Within himself, the sending of love, the intentional pursuit of relationship, was already taking place. Although words fail to perfectly capture the complexity of the Trinity, we can say that God, by nature, is a loving, sending God.

And if God is by nature a sending God, then what does that mean for the nature of his church? It means that infused into the very identity of God's people is sending DNA. Like him, the deepest inclination of our hearts is to be united to God and communing with one another in his loving mission. Needless to say, that's the kind of vision that can get the attention of every church member. It speaks to who they are, not simply what they do.

Don't worry, steps for the practical ministry of sending will soon come (remember, you've got sixteen chapters ahead of you). But if you're going to prioritize the church's culture before ministry, you must also prioritize identity before activity.

Made for More

Missions is notorious for being action-oriented. I remember consulting with a church that listed twenty-five different missional projects. They then presented them to their people as a form of "choose your own adventure." But only a small percentage of the church participated. Activity as a starting point will almost always fail to permeate a congregation. People are already exhaustingly busy. You'll never compete.

More significantly, projects alone do not appeal to people's souls, because they were made for more than projects. Let's return to the foundation that we've been building. God didn't just send his word to create a world and initiate a mission; he sent little reflections of himself to carry out that mission. This is what's happening when God crowns creation with a man and woman made in his image (Genesis 1:27), then blesses and commands them to be fruitful, multiply, fill the earth, subdue it, and have dominion over it (Genesis 1:28). In relationship with him, God entrusted humanity (an ever-growing global family) with his mission to fill the earth with his glory. This was the Great Mandate. It was a commissioning!

But what does it have to do with cultivating missions awareness? The Great Mandate is foundational for all that is to come in God's redemptive mission. It shows that when we are living out God's purposes of loving him and loving others, we are joining with God in filling the entire world with his glory. That work involves every church member and informs every part of their lives. You're awakening them to their "sent identity," their "sentness." This is their inherent calling as sent ones to their neighborhoods, as senders of fellow members to the nations, and, for some of them, as the missionaries who are sent.

You Are Sent

It goes like this. Each Sunday at a church where I pastored, the benediction ended with the same three words: "You are sent." Figuratively speaking, we were handing out those glasses again, helping them to see through a missional lens. We were reminding them of their birthright in God's mission. But that was only meaningful because the rest of the worship gathering had nourished them with the gospel. Yes, the Great Mandate is foundational, but what's ultimately served upon it is that delicious cake for which you've been preparing them.

Not long after humanity's first commissioning, through the sin of the first man and woman, we lost our capacity to carry out God's mission (Genesis 3:6–8). In time, fallen humanity would not only refuse to fill the earth with God's glory (Genesis 6:5), but they would also unite to twist the mission toward their own ends (Genesis 11:1–4). And yet God, being the loving, sending God that he is, continued to send.

He graciously revealed himself to people and sent them to participate in his mission again (think Noah sent to build the ark, Abram sent to the promised land, and Moses sent back to Egypt). He eventually redeemed a people, Israel, to be reunited to himself. He sent them laws to live by, the greatest of which was to love God with all their being and to love their neighbor as themselves. This would later be called the Great Commandment (Matthew 22:37–40). What exactly would it look like for people to once again be fruitful and multiply? It would look like loving God and loving neighbor.

And still God sent. Ultimately, he sent himself. How profound! Jesus Christ—God in flesh—came so that sinful humanity throughout the world could be fully and forever adopted by God (Galatians 4:4–5). His adopted children were entrusted with the mission once again, which is why Jesus says in John 20:21, "As the Father has sent me, even so I am sending you."

It's also why the Father and Son sent the Holy Spirit, and why the Father, Son, and Holy Spirit sent a new humanity on mission: the church. This mission is, of course, the Great Commission. What does it look like to be fruitful and multiply and to love God and neighbor? It looks like making disciples of all nations in communion with the Triune God and his sent people, an ever-growing global family. It means following in the way of Jesus, the true Sent One, by sacrificially embodying and proclaiming the gospel to those who have not yet heard, understood, and believed.

This is God saying with delight, "You are sent." In other words, go eat cake!

If it seems the metaphor is stretching too far, just consider the imagery we are given in the Book of Revelation. To participate in the final leg of God's mission is to prepare for the marriage supper of the Lamb (Revelation 19:6–8). There, disciples who have been made from every nation, tribe, people, and language will feast together. And get this: rather than all the sending coming to an end, instead it will return to its original, perfect expression of union and communion within the Triune God—*except that we will be caught up to participate in it forever.*

Look at that. The sending God from eternity past initiates the Great Mandate, the Great Commandment, and the Great Commission to ultimately seat us at his wedding table for eternity future.

And what do you eat at a wedding reception? Cake!

Apply Your Own Mask First

You are likely familiar with much of what we've just rehearsed. But it's worth rehearsing because it's the heart of your ministry. This seed, faithfully and patiently sown, will grow a people ready for missions awareness. There's only one thing left to do: apply your own mask first.

This is part of the instructions we hear just before every flight. "In case of emergency," says the flight attendant, "apply your own oxygen mask first before assisting others." Apparently, if you are frantically grappling with someone else's mask, you are more likely to pass out yourself. In that case, neither of you would make it! This scenario is similar to leading missions in the local church. You must first give attention to your own missiology before assisting others with theirs.

Notice, however, that I did not say your own missions *strategy*. Again, that will come soon. But first is missiology—the foundational study of God's mission. Many church missions leaders do not have missiological training or a missionary background. In truth, however, this can actually be advantageous *if* it leads you to take the posture of a learner. Over and over what we hear from people in our Upstream cohorts is how glad they are that they took time to invest in their own missiology. They studied the bigger picture of developing a sending church rather than giving in to the pressure for immediate results. In other words, they cultivated *themselves*. This is formation.

As you encourage the sent identity of every church member (and, hopefully, see some of them sent to other nations), you need to be the model for continuing to develop a missions heart. Read missiology. Think missiology. Live missiology. Here are a few practical examples of what I mean:

> » Read an introduction to missions such as *God's Heart*

for the Nations by Jeff Lewis.
» Learn about trends in global missions.
» Listen to cross-cultural voices and their perspective on the world.
» If you haven't traveled cross-culturally, get a passport and go visit a missionary—not to do a project, but simply to learn.
» Do a deep study of the church at Antioch in Acts 11–15.
» Research to see what people groups are in your area.

Above all, pray and ask the sending God to grow you. It will be the oxygen you need to lead others.

Baby Steps

When I first arrived as a missionary in East Africa, I was eager to share the gospel with everyone I met. The only problem was, I had to learn the language first. Interestingly, our method of language learning required being silent for at least the first month. I thought to myself, "How am I possibly going to speak the gospel fluently if I'm not even allowed to open my mouth?" This approach turned out, however, to be sheer brilliance. Forced to listen rather than blurt, I took in every tone and tenor of the dialect. Like an infant, I learned to hear the words and accent correctly. Then, at the end of that linguistically constipated month, I nearly burst with my first native-sounding words.

When you've worked hard to be "silent" and cultivate your own missions awareness first, you'll emerge bursting with readiness to mobilize church members. But before you focus entirely on that, consider this step: start with your church's leaders. If you go only to church members, then your influence may be limited. Instead, invest in the people whom God has called to guide the church. Depending on your role and the structure of your church, this may require you to "lead up," to influence the leadership of your church. Although it can feel like baby steps, any investment you make in your church's leaders can have massive returns. Capture the hearts of your senior pastor, elders, deacons, staff, and/or missions committee, and they might begin to see the whole church through the lens of sending too. Instead of approaching them to *get* something (like a bigger budget and more stage time), approach them to *give* something. You might do this by:

» Inviting them to eat with you at an international restaurant
» Offering a full or partial scholarship for them to go on a mission trip
» Giving them a copy of one of your favorite missiological books
» Sponsoring a group meal themed according to a particular country
» Providing missions-related resources relevant to a particular ministry
» Taking genuine interest in *their* cross-cultural experiences

Then, use the opportunity to cast some of the foundational truths we've discussed in this chapter. Share your desire to cultivate a sending culture. Feed *them* some cake!

They may be uninterested at first (hopefully, they don't sit on the cake like I did). But don't give up. Ask the sending God to move in their hearts in his time. Then, as you transition your attention to the wider church body, continue to find ways to encourage your leaders.

Giant Leaps

Now you're ready to engage the entire congregation. What's your first step? Stand on a box and sound forth the missionary call? Please don't. Instead, stand and sound forth God's loving, sending heart. It will call to the identity of every believer.

Even though the majority of people in your church will never be missionaries, this calling will be what moves them to reflect the sending God in two expressions: first, by living as "sent ones" who desire to participate in God's redemptive mission in their everyday lives; and second, by living as "senders" who are eager to commission and care for missionaries from their local church.

What does it look like to sound forth this call? Here are three important areas: teaching, prayer, and discipleship.

Cultivating Missions Awareness through Teaching

As the Book of Acts reveals all that Jesus continued to do through the Holy Spirit, we read of the church being established through devotion to the apostles' teaching (Acts 2:42). Amazingly, the words spoken in that day through the Holy Spirit carry the same "power of God for salvation" (Romans 1:16) when we speak them today. Just like a faithful missionary, why would we not start with God's Word?

Though some might call it an overemphasis, teaching Scripture with God's mission in mind is really just teaching Scripture faithfully. So find ways to get people into God's Word. Help them to see the foundational sending vision that we laid out earlier in this chapter.

If you have opportunities to preach, by all means leverage them well. Many people think missions is only emphasized in the Book of Acts. In reality, if you understand God as the sending God he is, then every word of Scripture points to his heart on mission—and our hands joining him. If you don't preach, encourage those who do to speak of God's heart for the world.

Here are a few other practical ways you can cultivate missions awareness through teaching:

> » Provide an easily accessible class that introduces people to God's mission, along with more advanced

34

opportunities like Perspectives on the World Christian Movement.

» Add a section to membership classes and material that explains sent identity.

» Visit each Sunday school class or small group to teach about the sending God and his sent people.

» Provide those who preach with missions resources: stories, graphics, research, missiological emphases in the book of the Bible they are preaching from, etc.

» Create a visually compelling missions display in a prominent area of the church building.

» Utilize your church's website and social media by posting content and videos that promote missions awareness.

» Develop a brochure or booklet that gives an overview of the sending church.

» Become a storyteller who always has thirty-second anecdotes that display life on mission.

Cultivating Missions Awareness through Prayer

Prayer may be second on the list, but it is just as important as teaching. If teaching is fuel for the fire, then prayer is what ignites and fans it into flame. This is clear in Paul's parting words to the elders at Ephesus: "'I commend you to God and the word of his grace, which is able to build you up and give you the inheritance among all those who are sanctified' . . . And when he had said these things, *he knelt down and prayed with them all*" (Acts 20:32, 36, emphasis mine).

When church leaders begin to pray for God's mission, the church will change. When church members begin to pray for God's mission, the world will change. Here we are reminded of Jesus's words in Luke 10. As he sends out his disciples to every place he is about to go, he acknowledges that the laborers in the harvest are few. We expect him to say something like, "So go and be those laborers!" Instead, he tells them as a matter of first importance,

"Therefore *pray earnestly* to the Lord of the harvest to send out laborers into his harvest" (Luke 10:2, emphasis mine).

In other words, pray to the sending God to send out his sent ones. After praying, the disciples then become the answer to their own prayer as they go on their way. What a beautiful example that can be just as impactful in your local church!

With that compelling vision in mind, here are a few practical ways you can cultivate missions awareness through prayer:

- » Pray for specific missions needs in Sunday worship services.
- » Pray for specific missions needs in Sunday school classes or small group gatherings.
- » Schedule regular missions prayer gatherings and include times of prayer in all missions events.
- » Teach through examples in Scripture of God using prayer to accomplish his redemptive mission.
- » Provide members with resources like *Operation World* by Jason Mandryk.
- » Distribute missionary prayer cards to all church members.
- » Develop a system for distributing immediate prayer needs from missionaries.

Cultivating Missions Awareness through Discipleship

The spirit of what we mean by the word "discipleship" is communicated in Upstream's first book, *Tradecraft: For the Church on Mission*. There, co-author Caleb Crider defines discipleship in the following way:

> The Christian life [requires] skill ... The conscious decision to deny oneself and follow Christ is a constant struggle that only becomes a habit through

practice. Prayer, fasting, taking a day of rest — these are learned behaviors that do not come naturally to most of us. These skills are honed through instruction, and are fostered to familiarity through repetition. Someone who has mastered the skill teaches it to those who need to learn the skill. Jesus called this discipleship.[1]

So, discipleship is more than teaching. Though the passing of information is important in the local church, if it doesn't apply to the heart and activate the hands, then it's simply education. But we must be warned that information without application can easily lead to hearing without doing (James 1:22) or knowledge without love (1 Corinthians 8:1). That will never make for a sending church.

Instead, as one sending church leader puts it, remember that experience drives education, not vice versa. Help your church members put their knowledge into action in order to cultivate missions awareness. What does that look like? Here are a few suggestions.

- » Define what you mean by the word "discipleship" and develop a basic framework for what it looks like in your context. (For example: "Discipleship is when an older Christian commits to personally show you how to be obedient to the commands of Christ.")
- » Invest in a group of church members in a reproducible way that allows them to become "missions mentors" to other church members.
- » Lead a group in reading through a book like *Tradecraft* or Scripture passages like Luke 10 and Acts 17, then take what you discussed and go practice it together in your town.
- » Establish a short-term mission trip (whether domestic or global) and disciple team members through all three phases of pre-field, on-field, and post-field. For more on this, see the Appendix's resource "Redeem-

ing Short-term Trips" or the Upstream book *Listen: How to Make the Most of Your Short-Term Mission Trip*.

» If you've never experienced missional discipleship that also prioritizes spiritual formation, check out a resource like *The Gospel-Centered Life* by Bob Thune and Will Walker.

And for more on this crucial task, the Appendix can direct you to our list of "Cultivating Missions Awareness Ideas," as well as a guide titled "Cultivating Missions Awareness Worksheet."

Sweet Delight

I'll never forget walking through a church building where nearly every ministry had the word "sending" in it: Sending Kids, Sending Youth, Sending Seniors. More than just language, leaders had structured these ministries to mobilize people on mission both locally and globally. People weren't just hearing about the sending God, they were experiencing their sent identity in structured, age-appropriate ways. The longer the church did this, the more a sending culture developed. It was like cake for everybody!

Of course, it may not be possible to overhaul your entire church to cultivate missions awareness. But every step you take toward it—every person you see awaken to sentness—can be a sweet delight.

This foundational task of Sending Church Element #1 will be more than just hustling for a small group of devotees to your ministry. It will be, in some sense, a missionary-like task: rooting deeply in a particular context, pointing people to God's heart, and leaving the results to him. It will not be easy. But it will form you and others more into the image of Christ.

How fun! How *profound*.

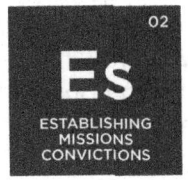

SENDING CHURCH ELEMENT #2: ESTABLISHING MISSIONS CONVICTIONS

By Bradley Bell

> *A sending church establishes missions convictions when it moves from general knowledge of God's mission to ownership of its own missional role. This depends primarily on the use of Scripture and prayer, so that the result is Spirit-filled rather than man-made. This also includes defining the church's particular missions convictions, which are a combination of the church's biblical convictions and its unique identity. These convictions then serve as a guide and filter for all of the church's missions activity.*

As I made the last brush stroke, it felt like the job was finally done. I had just spent the past week building a homemade basketball goal for a group of missionary kids. Playing sports was a rare treat in their part of the world, especially on an organized team. I thought they'd get a kick out of shooting some hoops every once in a while. Little did I know the ferocity that was coming my way—not unlike the attacking eagle I had just painted on the backboard.

These kids went basketball crazy. They wanted the full experience: practices, drills, conditioning, games. I figured once we slogged into the fundamentals they would calm down. Yeah right. They demanded uniforms. "Well, you can't have uniforms without a mascot," I told them, trying to counter the attack. It was no use. Without even a huddle they had decided: "We're the Flying Free Eagles!"

It was all my fault.

It Must Be

Conviction is a ferocious word that can carry two meanings. Generally, it refers to a strongly held belief. It's also used as a formal declaration that a person is guilty of a crime. In either expression, *conviction* has weight and grit. It's what we need to be firm and unmoving. When a bunch of missionary kids resolved to experience more than just a new backyard game, it revealed their conviction. They were ready for action.

I have heard it said that imagination is the belief that something *could be*. It's a vision of possibility. As we described in Chapter 1, cultivating missions awareness is giving believers the vision of a God who is rescuing people from all nations and who is sending us to participate. This eternity-past-to-eternity-future reality has the power to stir the soul and shape our identity. However, conviction goes further than this.

If imagination is the belief that something could be, conviction is the belief that it *must be*. It leads us to say, "God really can use me in his great global mission—*but I must act upon it.*" Conviction is what integrates the head and heart with the hands. It gets us moving, and it keeps us moving when the way gets tough.

The best example of this kind of conviction is Jesus himself. In Luke 9:51 we read, "When the days drew near for him to be taken up, he set his face to go to Jerusalem." This wasn't a matter of just visiting the great city. Jesus knew what would take place there in order to accomplish his redemptive mission. Surely in his humanity he experienced the human inclination to preserve his own life. Yet he resolved to press on, day after day. Now *that's* conviction.

Likewise, if a local church is to embrace more than missions awareness, there must be a similar resolve from the same source. Being "missions minded" is an excellent step—giving our money, prayers, and attention to lostness. But the path to becoming a sending church requires another step—giving *ourselves*. This means—by the power of Christ who lives in us—setting our faces toward our own unique missional role.

You Are Now Entering the Mission Field

You may have seen it when exiting a church. Often it's posted on the opposite side of a welcome sign. There are various versions, but one of the most common is this: "You are now entering the mission field." It's a way of giving all members a final nudge toward faithful witness. As was said at the church I pastored, "Remember, we are blessed to be a blessing."

Aside from whether or not such signs are effective, there is good reason for continually reminding people of the mission. We are consumers by nature, and modern culture only makes it worse. Hoarding knowledge without obedience comes quite naturally. Missions mobilizers are well aware of this ... and it drives us crazy.

Perhaps this is why mobilization tactics can so easily become law-based and guilt-motivated. Some examples include, "Don't you care about lost people?" and "If Christians had been obedient we would have already completed the Great Commission." Then there's the nightmare-inducing claim, "Their blood will be on your hands." These tactics certainly reflect the urgency of the matter and have a way of getting people's attention. The problem is that they use means that God himself does not use. In other words, when people are motivated by guilt, the results are man-made.

A Better Way

Sending Church Element #2 is not about finding ways to convict people, as though they are guilty of a crime. There is, after all, no longer any condemnation for those who are in Christ Jesus (Romans 8:1). Instead, this element is a matter of joining the Holy Spirit in establishing convictions—strongly held beliefs that lead to action. The two primary means of accomplishing this are Scripture and prayer.

This is how it seems the apostles articulated and exercised their leadership of the church. In Acts 6:4 we read that they installed deacons to carry out food distribution in order to "devote [themselves] to prayer and to the ministry of the word." This double emphasis was probably taken directly from the Lord Jesus, whose teaching clearly built on the Old Testament Scriptures and who spent extensive parts of his ministry in prayer. It certainly was the case for the church at Antioch, whose prophets and teachers worshiped, fasted, and prayed together, and in so doing encountered the sending God and became a sending church.

We heard of one local church that was inspired by this vision and decided to call for church-wide prayer and fasting. Following the lead of their pastors and staff, their people joined in. At the conclusion of the fast the church gathered for worship. It was then that something remarkable developed: a deep and unified conviction to abandon some old ways of doing things, and to become a church focused on sending. You can read the full story in their book, *The Sending Church: The Church Must Leave the Building* by Pat Hood.

Perhaps you would consider something similar; if not church-wide, then among your missions leaders. If nothing else, you personally can worship, fast, and pray in the ancient tradition of Antioch. Remember, many historical movements of God's mission began with intensive prayer.

Consider the Haystack Prayer Meeting of 1806, where a group of only five college students gathered to discuss the theology of missionary service but were interrupted by a thunderstorm. Taking shelter under a haystack, their forum turned into a prayer meeting. The experience would later be considered the catalyst not just for those students' missionary service, but for hundreds of others as well. Who knows what might happen at your church if you did something similar?

Following the Spirit

Ok, so maybe you won't start a missions movement. But God does not despise small things—especially when he gives birth to them. What we've been describing above is a church's conviction for missions that is Spirit-filled. It's for this reason that *Tradecraft: For the Church on Mission* kicks off by teaching the missionary skill of "following the Spirit."[1] There are thousands of missionary skills that could have been chosen, but this one was deemed the most foundational. Why? Because the Holy Spirit is how Jesus will finish what he started (Acts 1:1, 8).

When we consider the true enormity of God's mission, attempts to "finish the task" in our own strength may appear laughable. If reaching all the unreached people groups is the sole measure, then perhaps the Great Commission *can* be "completed." But if we take into consideration the missiological framework from Chapter 1, then God's mission requires more than evangelism. It includes making disciples in the context of local churches and baptizing believers who are taught to obey all that Jesus commanded— namely, to love God and neighbor (Great Commandment) in every part of life (Great Mandate). We are to seek this not just once in the history of each nation, but during every generation of every nation. That is truly overwhelming.

The point of all this is not to leave us in despair. Instead, it's meant to bring us to the end of ourselves and into desperate dependence on the Holy Spirit. When we admit that the mission is far beyond our means, but we still believe that the Holy Spirit will accomplish it through us, we are led to one foundational action: follow the Spirit!

Who are the people in your city that God has already prepared to receive the good news when they hear it? Follow the Spirit! What members is God calling your church to send cross-culturally? Follow the Spirit! Where exactly does God want you to send them? Follow the Spirit! How will you know when they have completed the work for which they were commissioned? You guessed it—follow the Spirit!

The Spirit Told Me

Of course, following the Spirit is both profoundly simple and surprisingly complex at the same time. Yes, the Spirit blows wherever he wishes (John 3:8), often confounding our human logic and desire. But there is a more troublesome factor involved: people.

Take, for instance, the strange narrative of Acts 21. Paul had resolved to go to Jerusalem, despite the Spirit testifying to him that imprisonment and afflictions awaited him (20:23). Along the way, the disciples at Tyre *through the Spirit were telling Paul not to go on to Jerusalem* (21:4, emphasis mine). Others, including a prophet, made the same plea. Still, he would not be persuaded, and his companions carried on saying, "Let the will of the Lord be done" (21:14).

So ... who was following the Spirit? We often assume whatever Paul did was right, but in this instance was he just being stubborn? Was the Spirit speaking different things to different people, or had they misunderstood him? Perhaps this was simply the messy process of people discerning the Lord's will. We're not sure.

Here's what is sure: we need one another's help in following the Spirit. Left to an individualistic mindset, it's easy to wield our personal preferences as Spirit-led convictions. Sometimes this looks like a person convinced of a very specific calling that he

44

has discerned on his own. Not only has he already determined all the details (where to go, what to do, when to leave, etc.), but he also expects the church to champion the ministry. Whether it's coming from a church leader or a church member, it can be difficult to argue with "The Spirit told me ..."

How then can a local church overflow with passion for sending without pouring itself into every personal preference? By establishing what we call "missions convictions."

A Sure Guide

If the Flying Free Eagles truly wanted to be a basketball team, they would need to know the rules of the game. Otherwise, their time on the court would just be organized chaos. So I painted lines and found a whistle, and I began to teach them the rules of the game (like not tackling the person with the ball). Eventually, they came to see why such guidance mattered.

Similarly, missions convictions serve as a guide for the church in following the Spirit. They are a combination of the church's biblical convictions and unique identity. Bethlehem Baptist Church in Minneapolis, Minnesota pioneered this idea in the early 1990s when they developed fourteen statements titled "Driving Convictions Behind Foreign Missions."[2] These convictions were then put before the church as a basis for their ongoing commitment to God's global mission.

Other sending churches have taken the concept further, not simply using it as a theological basis, but as a filter as well. In a world of tremendous need, there will be endless opportunities for missional activity. How will the church decide what to invest in? Will it prioritize church planting or humanitarian initiatives? Will it focus on supporting existing missionary partners or seek to send its own people? Will it aim to come alongside global church leaders or labor in places where there are none? The church's missions convictions can help leaders answer these questions with wisdom.

Imagine a beloved church member is in your office. Just a few months ago, she committed to establishing an orphan ministry in Uganda (where she has never been) and is on the cusp of quitting her job and selling her house. After an impressive presentation, her request to you is for the church to adopt her work and support it financially. Now, the Holy Spirit may be affirming that kind of partnership. But if he doesn't, how will you say "no" graciously without unnecessarily upsetting her and the congregation? The answer: your missions convictions.

In fact, you'll be able to give far more than a polite rejection. Missions convictions aren't just a bulwark that fortifies you against something. They are the specified beliefs that allow you to lead people toward a greater vision. For example, your response could sound something like, "We actually are passionate about sending our members on mission, but we want to do so in a way that fosters a reciprocal relationship between the field and the church, just like we see in Acts 13–14. Would you be interested in learning more about that process?" This is not a refusal. It's an invitation to discern the Spirit's leadership in the context of community. That's hard to beat!

Biblical Convictions

What exactly is the process for establishing these missions convictions? It begins with immersion in the Scriptures. What is the thread of global missions that runs from Genesis to Revelation? List out those key passages. Where do you see sending? Make special note of those sections. Pull up your church's doctrinal statement. Where do you see a basis for God's global mission? Perhaps there is an existing set of Scriptural core values at your church. Take those into consideration as well.

Some specific questions you might consider include,

> » What does your church think about the Great Com-

mission?

» Where do reached and unreached peoples come up in your priorities?

» How do you define missions and missionary?

Maybe think of it this way. A member of your church is in the process of being sent to a particularly dangerous part of the world. A few weeks before commissioning, you receive a letter from the candidate's parents demanding to know in detail why you would send them. What basis would you give from the Scriptures? Whatever you come up with, it would likely be similar to your biblical convictions for missions.

One thing to note: though there is much commonality between sending churches, biblical convictions are not universal when it comes to global missions. If they were, we'd include them here for you! Upstream works with numerous Christian denominations, and each one fosters slightly different emphases and applications of Scripture that are still faithful to orthodox Christianity. That's ok, and it demonstrates why it's important to work through this in your own context.

Unique Identity

After you have gathered information about your church's biblical convictions, you can give some thought to your church's unique identity. In his book *The 3D Gospel*, Jayson Georges suggests there are three different kinds of cultural identity: fear-power, honor-shame, and guilt-innocence.[3] In a predominantly guilt-innocence culture (which is the authors' cultural backgrounds), we are often subconsciously asking the question, "What is the right way?" This question assumes, of course, that there is only one right way to everything. Our background then urges us to find that way in order to bolster our identity and avoid being guilty.

When this cultural question is applied to our perspective of the local church—surprise!—it leads us to ask, "What is the right way to do church?" We certainly don't want to be guilty of doing it the *wrong* way! Of course, Jesus is the only right way to God. But where this "one way thinking" conflicts with establishing missions convictions is that every church does church a little bit (or a lot) differently. Every faithful church is unique—in context, history, gifting, resources, leadership, struggles, etc. Therefore, effective missions convictions must take into consideration a church's unique identity.

For example, the church where I pastored was planted with an aim of staying small and planting small, autonomous churches in order to place a high emphasis on deep relationships. Your church, on the other hand, may have been aimed at a city center that would then grow into multiple sites. A rural church may be passionate about discipling farmers, while a church in a college town aims for mobilizing students. Those differences are more than ok—they're *good*. In God's massive global vision, we need all these unique communal expressions of his kingdom.

So what makes your church unique? Don't be ashamed of it in comparison to others. Own it. Go with it. Write down your insights. Then combine them with your notes on biblical convictions. How do the two categories match up? What gets you most excited? Circle that. If you were to strip away almost everything, what would have to remain in order for your church to be who God meant for it to be? Highlight that. Getting too far out there into ideas and debates? Let your biblical convictions pull you back in.

As you go, begin to draw out particular statements that sum up a conviction. Ultimately, your goal will be to have eight to twelve of them. Once you've got those statements, unpack each of them in about a paragraph, including Scripture references. Here is an example:

> Because God pursues those who are far from him,
> we value mission among unreached and forgotten

peoples. (see Isaiah 49:1–6; Luke 5:30–32; and Romans 10:13–17, 15:20–21)

Although our temptation could become building a tower to the heavens with our church's logo on top (Genesis 11:1-9), we must fight to constantly look outward toward those far from us who do not know Jesus Christ. The "unreached" are those who have no one actively engaging them with the gospel. The "forgotten" are those who have been engaged in the past but among whom the gospel is no longer vibrant.

Of course, your missions convictions don't have to start like this one, but the basic framework might provide a good starting point. It might also be helpful to mention that such a sure guide is usually not developed overnight, nor in isolation. We encourage church leaders to take their time and to involve others in the process. We believe the Holy Spirit will honor this effort to seek his leadership in laying a healthy foundation for sending. And for more on this topic, see the Appendix, which can direct you to an "Establishing Missions Convictions Worksheet" and more "Examples of Missions Convictions."

Still Flying Free

Not long ago, one of those former missionary kids messaged me with an invitation to his wedding. You know what his first words were? "Hey, Coach Brad ..." Almost fifteen years later, he was still a Flying Free Eagle. Because those kids held to the collective belief that they could be a team, their lives were forever changed. If that can be true for intermediate basketball, then how much more for God's church?

I know there are likely great demands in your role for missions activity and results. Perhaps the thought of setting everything aside in order to focus on writing a document seems impossible or unhelpful. But as you'll see in the rest of the book, we will often return to this foundation. It *is* possible to develop a sending church without missions convictions, but doing so likely means you'll have to be the keeper of the conviction to send. The reality is, local church missions leaders aren't known for their longevity (they like to be on the move!). Establishing missions convictions, then, is a way of ensuring that sending not only happens but will continue on long after you.

In other words, it keeps your church flying free and set on following Jesus to the ends of the earth. It's worth it!

SENDING CHURCH ELEMENT #3: DEVELOPING A VISION

By Mike Easton

> *A sending church develops a vision when, building from its missions convictions, it writes a short and clear vision statement. This vision statement guides the church as it ultimately considers specific people, places, and/or projects in local and global missions. Although the vision is God-sized, the church encapsulates it in a simple and compelling statement that can be embraced by all of its leaders and members.*

A great gift to me as I began leading sending at my church was a clear and simple call from our lead pastor to "make sure global missions doesn't stink." How's that for a job description! While simple, the reason behind it was profound. We have such a great God—how can we not work hard to be both creative and excellent for his name?

What my lead pastor helped me to understand in that simple job description was that people are not always compelled by small things, and God is not honored when we put forth only minimal effort. God is honored and people are compelled by a vision that is more than we could ever ask for or imagine (Ephesians 3:20).

Think about your church's current global missions activity. Is it God-sized? Is it compelling? How could you make a lasting impact with your congregation to specific people, places, and/or projects—an impact about which you can say as a church, "God did it, and WE were a part of it"?

There will be a day when the ransomed from every nation, tribe, people, and language are standing before God's throne worshiping him for all of eternity (Revelation 7:9). Is your church's sending vision joining in on the work towards this promised reality? Let's jump into the process of developing this God-sized vision and see what the Lord might do.

Synergy

God has given each of us and our churches limited resources to steward. For everything we say "yes" to, we have to say "no" to something else. On the other hand, for everything we say "no" to, we have the opportunity to say "yes" to something else. It is poor stewardship to say "yes" to everything. Conversely, we would be missing out on opportunities if we said "no" to everything. A vision statement defines the borders for what we will say "yes" and "no" to. This is not only necessary for stewardship, but it is also necessary for group impact.

In this chapter and the next we will regularly refer to an important philosophy called "synergy." We can define synergy as "the interaction or cooperation of two or more organizations, substances, or other agents to produce a combined effect greater than the sum of their separate effects." This sounds very business-like, doesn't it? While we're not suggesting you operate your church like a business, we do want to offer some principles that we hope will help your church best cast the collective vision.

We see the benefits of synergistic work in many different endeavors. From architecture to engineering to sports to schools, those that work with synergy often make the greatest impact. Whether it's the building of the Pyramids of Giza, the settling of the Promised Land by the Israelites, the building of the Roman Empire, or winning the World Cup, great accomplishments all come through a group effort driven by a unified vision.

On May 25, 1961, American President John F. Kennedy gave one of the clearest vision statements of the twentieth century in his address to Congress. He said, "This nation should commit itself to achieving the goal, before this decade is out, of landing a man on the moon and returning him safely to the earth."[1] That short statement outlined a difficult but inspiring vision. It defined a timeline for its accomplishment. It garnered public sentiment, mobilized its nation's resources, and employed over 100,000 people. President Kennedy set in motion a goal that would outlive his direct influence and be accomplished six years after his untimely death.

Churches, more than any other group, have a great foundation for this kind of synergistic impact. The church gathers under the most important vision in the universe: the shared vision of Jesus Christ being exalted around the world and his people finding their joy in him forever. We have the common identity of belonging to his universal church. We also have the collective membership in a local church body in which we grow and go with the gospel. What a foundation!

However, in order to actualize our potential as local churches, we need to define our unique vision. In the last chapter, we discussed establishing missions convictions. These convictions are formed by what you believe the Bible says about missions and also your unique identity as a church. With those convictions in mind, you have the foundation for creating a God-sized and compelling vision of sending for your church. When this vision is regularly and clearly put before your people, you do not simply make an individualistic impact—you make a synergistic impact on the world.

As more and more church members buy into the vision, you will see exponential impact over what just one individual can do.

Collective vs. Individual

Unfortunately, when I survey a church for what they are engaged in globally, I rarely find synergistic reasons for their endeavors. Instead, what I often observe is individual members having a vision for missions and bringing it to the church. The church then adds this idea to their menu of missions giving and opportunities for their people.

When we look at the Scriptures, however, we see little individualism in missions sending. Consider the example of the church at Antioch. It is much more collective in its origin and activity than what many modern churches are practicing. In Acts 13:1–3 we read,

> Now there were in the church at Antioch prophets and teachers, Barnabas, Simeon who was called Niger, Lucius of Cyrene, Manaen a lifelong friend of Herod the tetrarch, and Saul. While they were worshiping the Lord and fasting, the Holy Spirit said, "Set apart for me Barnabas and Saul for the work to which I have called them." Then after fasting and praying they laid their hands on them and sent them off.

We are going to refer to the example of the church in Antioch throughout this book. In this particular section of their story, there is a collective nature to the church-wide recognition of calling, which then leads to the sending of a team.

This makes me think of a game called "Total Chaos." Imagine 150 people, divided into two teams, coming together on a small playing field. Instead of playing one sport with one ball, you're playing three sports with multiple balls and objects, and all at the same time! Soccer, ultimate frisbee, and football games are happening simultaneously on the same field.

While this is a super fun game, after an hour of literal total chaos, you are completely physically and mentally wiped out. Not only are you running the entire time, but you're also having to decide at each moment whether to chase the football, defend the soccer ball, or throw the frisbee to someone, all while looking around for whatever object might be heading in your direction. It's fun, but it's also a little maddening.

Similarly, in churches we are too often playing different games on the same field. It might look like we're making missions progress, but the lack of structure and strategy means our activity might be more chaotic than we would like to admit. Developing a missions vision helps align members with the unique calling God has on your church for synergistic impact.

Developing a Vision Statement

Over the rest of this chapter and into the next, we are going to work through what it looks like to create a vision, values, and strategy document. This document will give direction for your church's leadership as they steward the resources of your church towards kingdom impact.

A vision statement tries to help an organization answer the questions "Why do we exist?" and "Where are we headed?" Your local church likely has a vision statement that broadly answers these questions. Below are vision statements we gathered from three different churches (for more, see the Appendix's "Developing a Vision Examples"):

Church #1 - *For the City. For the Campus. For the Glory of God.*

Church #2 - *To reach people with the gospel, build them up as a church, and send them to the world.*

Church #3 - *Worship and glorify God—love and disciple people—reach and serve the world.*

You see in each church vision statement why they exist and what their church is trying to accomplish. Vision statements must be memorable. Your tendency will be to spell everything out in a vision statement. However, memorability must win the day. There will be opportunities to flesh out more specifics in the values and strategy. But for now, ask yourself, "What does the average member need to know and remember?" These three churches do a great job of defining the vision succinctly. And knowing each of these churches, we're sure every word in these vision statements was discussed at length.

Why start with the church's vision? Because, as we mentioned in Chapter 1, "Cultivating Missions Awareness," sending locally and globally isn't a department of the church—it is a church-wide vision that starts with the leaders of the church. While having a sending or missions department is helpful for developing partnerships locally and sending members cross-culturally, sending should be built into every aspect of the church. From your vision statement to programs to Sunday mornings, each aspect should have sending as the end goal. It's possible that you need to re-evaluate your church's vision statement with your leadership team to more accurately reflect your desire to send as a church.

Whether you consider local and/or global sending as a department, program, or process, the vision statement of global sending should flow from—not against—your vision as a church. Therefore, when you create a vision statement for global sending, it can be a helpful part of the exercise to write down your church's vision and preface it with, "as an overflow of our church's vision, our sending vision is to ..."

Going back to the three churches I mentioned earlier, here's how they did it:

Church #1 - *Our church exists "For the City. For the Campus. For the Glory of God." As an overflow of our church's vision, our global sending vision is to "Send out healthy members and resources to catalyze Gospel Church Movements in global university cities with low access to the gospel."*

Church #2 - *At our church, our vision is "To reach people with the gospel, build them up as a church, and send them to the world." As an overflow of our church's vision, our global sending vision is to "send healthy members to multiply disciples and churches in international cities."*

Church #3 - *At our church, our vision is to "Worship and glorify God—love and disciple people—reach and serve the world." As an overflow of our church's vision, our global sending vision is to "partner in evangelism, church planting, and pastor training. Our hope is that by strategically partnering with missionaries and ministries that focus on one or more of these areas, we might participate in the broadening and deepening of God's church around the world."*

As you can see, each church made some effort to tie their global sending vision to their overall vision as a church.

Now it's your turn! Here's an exercise to help you and a group of leaders within your church develop your own vision statement:

1. Pray - It can go without saying, but I want to say it: pray! Pray in preparation for this meeting. Pray at the beginning of this meeting. Pray during the meeting. Pray after the meeting to ask the Lord to confirm your vision statement. Invite the leading of the Holy Spirit to work through this unique group of people for the sake of your church and its mission.
2. Brainstorm - Write a list of ten to fifteen words that stick out to you from your convictions. Put them on a white-

board or tear sheet visible to the group.

3. Narrow Your List - Ask each member of the group to choose three words they think are most important to include in your vision statement. Put a check mark next to each of those words. Which six words have the most checks? Ernest Hemingway was once challenged to write a story in six words. He wrote, "For sale, baby's shoes, never worn."[2] That six-word story drives the emotions and the imagination. Could your missions vision be that short and still drive the hearts, the emotions, and the actions of your people?

4. Form Your Statement - From that list of six words, form your vision statement. Add the right grammar to make the sentence flow correctly, but try to stick to those six nouns or verbs you voted upon.

5. Revise Your Vision Statement - Take time to think through the implications of this vision statement. If needed, pull in some of the words from your larger list and revise it. Are there any partnerships you currently have as a church that you would have to say "no" to because of this global sending vision? Does the vision help you say "yes" to people, places, and/or projects your church would like to say "yes" to?

6. Try It On - Before buying clothes, we typically consider the type of fabric, the size, the fit, and the purpose of the clothes. As a team, you need to take the vision to the "dressing room." Try it on for a week or two. Ask team members to consider what they like and do not like about the vision statement and come back together to finalize it.

7. Be Flexible - Undoubtedly, you will need to change your vision in the future. You may even need to do an overhaul every five to ten years. But at this point you have something written down that is agreed upon by the group and that can be lived out as you make decisions

for the church in sending.

For more help with this critical process, the Appendix can direct you to our "Developing a Vision Worksheet."

Values

Before finishing this chapter I want to address an important link between Element #3, "Developing a Vision," and Element #4, "Building a Strategy." It is the importance of values.

Values ask the question, "What do we want to be known for?" When people look at your sending vision, the strategy, the missionaries, the partners, and the senders, what should be true of them? Here are a few questions to consider when forming a list of values:

» Are you going to have a spread-out or focused approach in global sending? If you are more focused in your approach, you might consider values like *focused*, *strategic*, or *stewardship*.

» Is it a high value for your church to be focused on teams, locations, and initiatives that your members, home or abroad, are already or will be a part of? If so, you might consider values such as *member-driven* or *member-empowering*.

» Do you want to be known for being exceptional at missionary care? If so, then you might consider values like *shepherding*, *relational*, *healthy*, or *care*.

» Are you wanting to be known for cutting-edge, frontier ministry work? Then you might consider values like *ambitious*, *apostolic*, *pioneering*, or *frontier*.

» Think about your disposition towards your partners. What do you want your church to be known for regarding the way you treat your senders, your missionaries, and your partners? You might consider values such as *generous, strategic, focused,* and *empowering.*

Returning once again to the examples of the three churches from earlier, here's how their vision statements then led to identifying values:

Church #1:

» Strategic - We will follow the leading of the Holy Spirit to choose our targets slowly, wisely, and strategically.
» Generous - We will work hard to catalyze and partner generously with other churches.
» Healthy - While being ambitious, we will prioritize the health of our missionaries and teams over expansion.
» Focused - We will decide what we Own, Catalyze, and Bless [explained in the next chapter] based on the degree to which the partnership involves our people or people we like, strategic places, and the types of strategic projects in which we want to involve our-selves.

Church #2:

» Relentless Mission - We actively engage in God's global mission and are willing to sacrifice for it.
» Intentional Mobilization - Robust assessment and development of pre-field missionaries.
» Proactive Care - Intentional and ongoing missionary care.
» Teaming - All aspects of missions are done within the context of a team.

Church #3:

> » Focused - We don't give where we don't go.
> » Generous - We are generous with our resources.
> » Member-Driven - We prioritize partnerships with missionaries and ministries that arise from within our church body.

It's clear that each church made an effort to spell out what really matters to them. This then prepared them well for moving from vision to strategy.

Now you try. Similar to the steps you took with developing a vision statement as a team, develop your values.

1. Brainstorm a smaller list of four to eight words that reflect the characteristics and qualities for which you want to be known. At this point, try to avoid strategic words or specific ministry projects. We'll get to that in the chapter on strategy.
2. Narrow your list by having each member vote for one or two values they think are most important.
3. Define each value.
4. Take a week or two to try on the values for size and fit.
5. Finalize that list.

This list now represents what you want to be known for, and what you want to be true of yourselves as a church. May the Lord make it true of you!

Global Missions That Doesn't Stink

I'm thankful for the simple job description my lead pastor gave me to make sure our global missions vision is God-sized. As a missions leader, I know you want the same. We have one life to live, and we want to make the greatest impact we can. Developing a vision will help a church maximize its impact in its own life cycle.

It is important for churches to pause and think strategically about who they want to be and what they want to be about in sending. Developing a vision takes patience and courage, but we believe it will lead your church toward having a greater eternal impact. Go for it!

SENDING CHURCH ELEMENT #4: BUILDING A STRATEGY

By Mike Easton

> *A sending church builds a strategy by creating a clear sending process for the church to ultimately fulfill its vision. The sending process creates a mobilization strategy for short-, mid-, and long-term missionaries. This strategy then gives direction to the impact missionaries are expected to have, including a budget that reflects sacrificial giving and intentional planning.*

The 2023 Denver Nuggets were a unique NBA championship team. Their front office took ownership of a traditionally under-performing organization and slowly built a team over the course of seven years with the vision to win an NBA championship. Their strategy was to build the team with players that not only had great skill but were also fully committed to one another. They were selfless, had a low ego, learned to play together, and bought into a greater vision.

Their star, Nikola Jokic, a two-time NBA MVP, was not a flashy, boisterous player, but he was an incredible facilitator. When asked if he was the best player on the team, he said, "Sometimes I am. Sometimes I'm not. I'm cool with that. And I think everyone else is good with that."[1] This is a rare statement from a millionaire superstar who, at the time, was clearly the best player on his team. Furthermore, his teammate Jamal Murray, when asked about his in-game accomplishments, regularly deflected praise to his teammates. In an era where ego is often celebrated, it was refreshing to see humility and teamwork win the title.

As we move to the next element of a sending church, humility and teamwork are going to lead you to accomplish great things as well. In Chapter 3, "Developing a Vision," we shared the importance of setting a clear vision for your church to get everyone's sights on where they are going. In this chapter we want to talk about how to implement this vision for kingdom impact. This implementation of a vision is known as the "strategy."

How to Accomplish a Vision

Vision and strategy are really two sides of the same coin. When one is lacking, there is little impact. When there is a great vision but no strategy, people get excited but do not actually do anything. When there is a great strategy but no vision, there may be a lot of busywork, but no eternal impact is made.

The greatest sports teams have both a vision and a strategy, which they implement through teamwork and selflessness. But vision and strategy should not be limited to sports teams and businesses. Long-time pastor David Horner says,

> Rather than embrace a noble vision and then attempt to pursue it in a haphazard manner, churches need a strategic approach to their efforts that takes into consideration not only the vision itself but also the purposes, principles, and values of the

congregation as a whole. A strategy provides both
a logic and a first level of detail for how a vision
can be accomplished.[2]

As believers, the call to selflessness is inherent to who we are because of the one we follow, Jesus Christ. We have the vision to see Christ exalted among the nations, and as missions leaders, it's our job to take the vision God has given the church universal, as well as the unique vision of our local church, and implement a strategy that will have a kingdom impact for eternity.

Strategy answers the question "How do we accomplish the vision?" Relating back to basketball, the greatest teams "follow the play." That means everyone is moving around the court to the right place at the right time, and they are either taking the shot when they are supposed to, passing, screening, rebounding, sitting on the bench, coaching, or executing whatever their role may be. When an individual decides not to follow the play, the team crumbles and their impact goes unrealized.

It is the role of the leadership in the church, under the guidance of the Holy Spirit, to provide not only the vision but also the strategy in sending. It is the role of the church member, while providing feedback to their leadership, to follow the vision and strategy of the church. By God's grace, when church leaders stick to their vision and strategy, invite and motivate their people towards that vision and strategy, and listen to the feedback of their members on that vision and strategy, the churches they serve will make a great impact.

Calling the Play to Run

Defining a clear strategy gives specificity to "the play" you want your church members to run. By forming it you are asking what specific people, places, and/or projects you want to focus on. You are defining the borders of what partnerships you do or do not pursue. Some questions you might consider when formulating your strategy are:

» People - Who do we want to partner with locally and globally? Do we only partner with those who are members of our church? How do we decide when to partner with someone outside of our church?

» Place(s) - Are there any particular strategic locations in our community or around the world that we want to focus on? Are we drawn to locations that are urban or rural, reached or unreached, high or low development? Why?

» Project(s) - Are there particular types of ministry we want to be a part of, such as church planting, pastor training, Bible translation, short-term trips, justice work, youth camps, etc.? Why?

With these questions in mind, now consider the following exercise with your leadership team:

1. Make a list of five to ten strategies as you answer the above questions about People, Place(s) and Project(s). Write a one- or two-word title for every strategic point and give a short description of each.

2. Rank that list. One way to rank lists like these is to have each member of the decision-making team choose two strategies they think are most important. Then reorder the list based on the votes cast.

3. Cut the list down to three to five key strategies and reorder based on discussion.

Here are some examples of this exercise from the three churches I referred to in the previous chapter:

Church #1	Church #2	Church #3
Church Planting	Persecuted Church	Evangelism
Unreached	Church Planting	Pastor Training
University Students	Bible Translation	Mobilizable Areas
Church Strengthening	Member Involvement	Orphan Care
Member Involvement	Short-Term Trips	

Once you have completed that exercise and have your own list, dive a little deeper into the descriptions and subpoints of each strategy. There is a wide range of thoughts on what "church planting," "serving the persecuted church," or "pastor training" actually means. In subpoints, get specific on the type of ministry you would like to see happen in your sending efforts. Take "church planting," for example. It would be valuable to further specify that strategy based on the following list of questions:

> » Is there a particular church planting model our partners need to follow?
> » What type of leadership structure do those we partner with need to have?
> » Do we expect leaders of churches to be indigenous believers?
> » Is there a particular theological viewpoint they need to follow? If not, are there theological borders that we will maintain in our partnerships?

The process of aligning your missions efforts around a strategy will take time. Be patient with your leadership team as you develop your strategy. Plan on opportunities to revisit it. At minimum, get something down on paper that has been developed in community. Try it on. Live it out and make adjustments as you grow.

Building a Focus and Funding Model

A key part of implementing a strategy for sending is building a focus and funding model. This defines how much attention, time, energy, and resources will be given to particular partnerships. As a church you will look for partners that help you fulfill your strategic objectives. These partnerships will be with individuals or organizations in local or global contexts.

Locally, these partnerships may be with members of your church or other believers outside of your church looking to meet particular needs in your community. Globally, these partnerships may be with members sent from your church, other missions leaders from your country, and/or indigenous believers or organizations with a similar vision and strategy.

Although a strategic focus, funding model, and partnership grid may seem more secular than spiritual, giving attention to these things is ultimately about stewarding our God-given resources. Stewardship is an important calling in Scripture and something missions leaders are entrusted with in the life of a church. This comes out clearly in the Parable of the Talents from Matthew 25:14-30.

The Parable of the Talents is not only a warning for what happens when you are not a good steward. It also gives us a vision of what can happen when you are! As you are probably familiar, in it Jesus describes a man who goes on a journey and gives various amounts of money to each of his servants in order for them to make a profit. Two of the servants steward their money well and multiply it for their master, but one of them simply buries his in the ground. The two receive a reward while the one incurs wrath. And we as readers walk away challenged to steward well what has been loaned to us from God as we await the day of accounting at Christ's return.

While this passage doesn't include a specific command to the church, we know faithful stewardship needs to characterize how the church uses members' time and finances. As missions leaders we have the opportunity to direct our stewardship towards a particular vision and strategy that will have a multiplying effect—or to bury it in the ground. I know you're reading this book because you do not want to bury those resources in the ground. You want to see them multiply!

In my first two years of being the missions pastor at my church, I kept a list of all the snail mail, e-mails, and phone calls I received from people around the world asking for partnership. In those two years, I received partnership requests from people or organizations in over half of the countries in the world! As I received those emails and phone calls, I often felt a level of anxiety rise in me. I'd wonder, "How am I going to say no to this organization? They may be doing great work. I don't want to offend them. Even if I say no, will they understand why?" You can see that I had some people-pleasing issues to work out in my life!

After those first two years, as the strategy was clarified by our leadership (and I worked on my emotional health), I no longer dreaded those fundraising meetings. I had a clear filter in my mind for what we were aiming for as a church, which I could then communicate to that person asking for partnership. While leaving room for the Holy Spirit to work, I was able to go through those meetings with clear objectives and clearly communicate our strategy to those asking for partnership.

Having a vision and strategy gave our missions team clarity about what we were working towards. As a result, our team was able to mobilize many people to implement the strategic goals our leadership had set out.

Own, Catalyze, and Bless

How do you determine which partnerships will help you best steward your people's focus and funding? With all your partnerships in mind, with which should you have a higher or lower investment? One framework for discerning focus and funding towards a partnership is evaluating how well the partnership's people, places, and projects align with your vision and strategy. Consider these the "three P's."

1. People - This includes members of your church that you have sent and/or connects with people you have come to know and love.
2. Places - This includes locations of the people you want to reach.
3. Projects - This includes ministry endeavors that fit your vision and strategy.

The idea is, the more of the three P's the partnership includes, the more focus and funding they will receive. It is a very simple way to quickly gauge whether you should say "yes" or "no" to a person or organization raising funds.

A helpful way to complete this exercise is to create tiers of focused funding based on how many of the P's the partnership includes. These tiers are helpful for efficiently communicating your level of investment in each partnership. In his book *Gaining by Losing,* J.D. Greear gives some helpful names for these tiers: Own, Catalyze, and Bless.[3] I will add definitions of each based on how they relate to the three P's:

1. Own - These are partnerships that include all three P's. They involve your members and are in a place where the people you want to reach live. The project aligns with your strategy, and you take great ownership in its implementation as a church.
2. Catalyze - These are partnerships that include two of the three P's—people and either a place or a project. The idea for this partnership will likely come from a person in your church or an organization you like. You help the endeavor happen but do not have direct responsibility for it.

3. Bless - These are partnerships that include one of the three Ps—likely people, but possibly a place or a project you will love and get behind. Most likely you are partnered because of a member's involvement. While you want to cheerlead the work God is doing through that member, the partnership will receive minimal focus and funding because of the limited degree to which your church can be involved.

Determining these tiers of partnership will give you and your leadership team the ability to make decisions around focus and funding for new and existing partners more quickly and efficiently. It also serves as a way to be clear with partners about your level of involvement and why. Partnerships respect and prefer clarity.

Let's make this really practical. Try out the following exercise with your team:

- » Create a table like the one below.
- » List all your partners on the vertical axis.
- » List all your strategies on the horizontal axis.
- » Weigh your strategies between 1 and 10. The closer a strategy is to 10, the more critical it is. A strategy that is closer to 1 may still be important, but it carries less weight. The weight will serve as the highest score that a strategy can receive.
- » Go through each partner and give them a score for how well they fulfill each strategy.
- » Total up the "scores" for each partnership.
- » Give a score for how much focus your people give towards that partnership.
- » Include how much money you give per month or per year to that partnership.

Here is an example of what this exercise might look like:

Partner	Church Planting	Unreached	Sent from our Church	Justice & Mercy Ministry	Recieve ST Trips	Total Score		Current Focus	Current Funding
Score	Up to 10	Up to 8	Up to 6	Up to 4	Up to 2	Up to 30		Up to 10	Add $$
Partner 1	10	8	6	4	2	30		3	$250/month
Partner 2	3	7	4	4	2	20		5	$500/month
Partner 3	4	3	5	3	0	15		9	$1,000/month

After you have given a score in each of the strategic categories for each of your partners, do the following:

> » Rearrange your partnerships by score.
> » Discuss what you notice about the investment given to each partnership in terms of focus and funding.
> » As a team, evaluate if the resources you are investing in each partner align with their score in comparison to other partners.

If you find that a partnership you give very little focus and funding to scores high (like Partner 1), maybe you should add some focus and funding to that partnership. If a partnership scores low (like Partner 3), but you're giving lots of focus and funding to that partnership, you will need to consider lowering the amount given to them.

A final step you can take is to categorize the rearranged partners by Own, Catalyze, or Bless (or come up with your own names for your tiers). This will all take work, but the clarity it brings is worth it—not to mention the good stewardship!

Funding Partners

Now let's consider how this could look in your church's budget. The following table has some examples of how a church might determine funding for individuals, families, or organizations based on each tier per month. The numbers and percentages will differ from church to church. The point is to decide what your minimums, maximums, and percentages would be.

Own	Minimum		Maximum	Recommendations
Individuals	$500	to	$700	15-20% of missionary's budget
Families	$750	to	$1750	15-20% of missionary's budget
Organizations	$2,000	to	$5,000	
Catalyze				
Individuals	$150	to	$250	5-10% of missionary's budget
Families	$250	to	$500	5-10% of missionary's budget
Organizations	$250	to	$1,000	
Bless				
Individuals	$50	to	$100	$50-$100/month
Families	$100	to	$200	$100-$200/month
Organizations	$100	to	$250	

Categorizing your partnerships in tiers like this will help guide the leadership of the church as they highlight partnerships and draw your people to them. For each tier of Own, Catalyze, and Bless, you'll want to consider some of these questions regarding the use of your people's time in relation to that partnership:

>> If individuals want to be sent by your church, how much time and energy will you give them in the sending process based on their tier?
>> What communication platforms will you give partnerships? Consider areas such as stage time on Sunday morning, small groups, equipping ministries, etc.
>> To which tiers of partners will you send short-term trips?
>> How much attention will you give partners in various tiers on the field for shepherding, resourcing, and care?

There is way more to this process than we can cover in a single chapter. So, check out the Appendix for a resource called "Focus & Funding Model Development Explained," along with a "Budgeting Template."

Spirit-Led Strategy

The word "strategy" can feel like the antithesis of being "Spirit-led." If done improperly, it can be more "of man" than "of the Spirit." We addressed this topic in Chapter 2, but in the midst of such a practical chapter it's worth revisiting.

Being *Spirit-led* is often equated with *spontaneity*, and being *of man* is often linked with *planning*. This is an unnecessary dichotomy. One can be *planned* and *Spirit-led* as well as *spontaneous* and *Spirit-led*. Conversely, one can also have *planning* that is *of man* and *spontaneity* that is *of man*.

The goal of forming a strategy is to come to an agreed-upon set of principles that, as Bradley Bell says in Chapter 2, provide a "filter" for making your decisions as a church. But churches need to be careful that these filters don't move from guidelines to rigid policies. We must stay in step with the Spirit when implementing our strategies. We make changes and exceptions to the strategy as needed, especially as the Spirit leads us in ways that fall outside our original plans.

The greatest accomplishments in world history had a plan that garnered the support of many to a singular, fantastic vision. The Denver Nuggets had a vision and strategy, and it gained them fame, fortune, and an earthly prize. How much greater is the prize we seek: the glory of God among the nations!

Church leaders, lead your people to work together toward the promised vision of the ransomed from every nation, tribe, people, and language worshiping before God's throne. There is no greater work toward which we could give our time, energy, and resources!

SENDING CHURCH ELEMENT #5: INVOLVING THE ENTIRE CHURCH

By Bradley Bell

"

A sending church involves the entire church by clearly and consistently teaching its missions convictions, vision, and strategy. This is done in such a way that every member understands their roles and opportunities to participate in God's mission through the church. This also includes developing an infrastructure of missions leaders who help execute the sending process.

One of the clearest examples in the New Testament of a church on mission is that of the church in Ephesus. Michael T. Cooper, author of *Ephesiology*, describes it as "the most significant movement in the history of Christianity."[1] Many of us have come to love the rich ecclesiology of Paul's letter to the Ephesians, but the fuller story of the church's history is told in Acts 18–20. There, through the combined efforts of Apollos, Paul, Priscilla, and Aquila, the Holy Spirit gave birth to a new church. Though that is a miracle in itself, we're then stunned to read this in 19:8–10:

And [Paul] entered the synagogue and for three months spoke boldly, reasoning and persuading them about the kingdom of God. But when some became stubborn and continued in unbelief, speaking evil of the Way before the congregation, he withdrew from them and took the disciples with him, reasoning daily in the hall of Tyrannus. This continued for two years, so that all the residents of Asia heard the word of the Lord, both Jews and Greeks.

All of Asia Minor encountered the gospel in two years?! It's hard to fathom. However, the way we often try to explain it centers on Paul's preaching—we assume all those people came to hear him preach. But in reality it was the *impact* of Paul's preaching that spread, and it spread through the vessels of people. The entire church was involved in the mission.

How might that happen in your church?

Slow-Brew Missions

Chapter 1, "Cultivating Missions Awareness," introduced the importance of building a sending culture rather than a missions ministry. A missions ministry focuses on the busyness of missions activity rather than the anchor of sent identity. When the church is taught that projects are where the church's mission begins (and, perhaps, ends), only a limited number of church members will get involved. A programmatic approach then depends on the same few people who pray, give, and go. Thus, it rarely involves the entire church.

By contrast, it takes time and intentionality to cultivate each member's sent identity. This is their inherent calling as sent ones to their neighborhoods, as senders of fellow members to the nations, and, for some of them, as the missionaries who are sent. But when churches do this hard identity work, it forges a sending culture, resulting in a more consistent stream of activity that grows out of a collective vision.

Let's use a coffee analogy to describe the difference between these two approaches of church involvement. Think of a missions ministry versus a sending culture as an espresso shot versus a pour-over.

The Espresso Shot

The espresso shot is a quick and intense cup of coffee. It only takes a minute to make it with a machine. In some coffee shops, an espresso is automated and the machine does it for you. You simply push a button, and after a few seconds, out pours an espresso.

Of course, a quality shot of espresso takes intentionality to turn out well. It is important to get the right grind for the coffee and to tamp the grounds properly. The barista has to skillfully "dial in" such a focused burst of flavor—not too bitter, acidic, or sour. The result is a caffeinated punch that gives you a boost for the next hour.

In this analogy, an espresso shot is like a short-term mission trip, which tends to be the primary activity of a missions ministry. In today's world, short-term mission trips can almost be automated. Their results can be pretty predictable as well—those who go often return with a sense of participation in God's global mission (and the church has the opportunity to adopt that sense of participation as well).

Of course, a *quality* short-term mission trip certainly cannot be automated. It takes planning, strategy, and experience to support the work of long-term missionaries, allowing the fruit from the trip to continue being harvested long after the team is gone. However, even when executed well, the "caffeinated punch" usually only impacts the church for a short period of time. The missions ministry then depends on answering the question, "So, when is the next trip?" The church gets the sense that they're only on mission when they're on a plane to another country.

The Pour-Over

Another side of this analogy is the pour-over. It is art and science combined. A pour-over requires the right amount of perfectly ground coffee, measured to the gram on a scale. It also requires the right amount of water, heated to and maintained at the perfect temperature. Even the empty filter is wet with hot water (to avoid affecting the flavor) and the pot is pre-heated with hot water (to avoid affecting the temperature). The fresh grounds are then slightly wetted and allowed to rest for about thirty seconds to facilitate certain chemical reactions. Finally, you slowly pour the remaining water over the grounds at a controlled rate. The result is a perfectly brewed pot of coffee that lasts throughout the morning.

This analogy relates to the idea of establishing a sending culture. See how much more work goes into the final product? Getting missions to permeate the entire church cannot happen only through short bursts of activity. It requires "filtering" every aspect of the church through a missional lens. It includes a slow, constant "drip" of sending theology and vision into every ministry.

Though the sending culture may take more time and effort to establish, its results are much longer lasting. For example, a sending culture provides multiple on-ramps to missions involvement *before* a person ever goes on a short-term mission trip. Then, it also provides multiple next steps *after* the mission trip besides just going on another trip. All these steps are aimed at helping each participant learn to think and act like a missionary in every setting of life, whether local or global. That's a powerful brew!

The Americano

Ok, let's stretch the coffee analogy just a bit further. Is there a way to get the best of both worlds—espresso and pour-over? The closest thing to that is called the Americano. It is made by diluting espresso with hot water until it has a similar strength to (though a different flavor from) the pour-over. For the person who wants both the punch of an espresso and the strength of a pour-over, the Americano is the way to go.

Here, the analogy applies to the church that wants to kick-start its sending culture. One of the most effective ways to do this is to take multiple key leaders—including the lead pastor—on a vision trip. Seek out a trusted missionary, church planter, or global church leader (ideally someone with whom you'd like to partner in a place in which you'd like to invest). Go and immerse yourselves in that context for a week or so. Think and act like missionaries. Catch God's sending vision.

Then come home and begin following the elements laid out in this book. Although much foundational work will still need to be done, you will likely have a more caffeinated beginning. In addition, leveraging key leaders from the outset will create ownership and spread influence. That's certainly a kick-start to involving the entire church.

Clear and Consistent Teaching

So, after pausing this chapter to get yourself an *actual* espresso, pour-over, or Americano, what's the first practical step you can take toward filtering all of your church members through your sending culture? It relates to the avenue that most consistently influences every member: teaching. I'm not talking about teaching on missions in general (see Chapter 1). I'm talking about teaching what you've already worked to produce: your missions convictions (see Chapter 2), vision (see Chapter 3), and strategy (see Chapter 4). Let me explain.

Teaching Missions Convictions

Your missions convictions combine your church's biblical convictions and unique context to clarify what motivates and guides your church in missions. Think of them like a foundation on which you build, a set of guardrails that keep you on track, a colander through which everything is filtered. You don't want to keep them to yourself—you want to take every opportunity to teach them formally and informally. Here are a few ways you can do that:

» Work them into any missions event you have. If it's a short event (like a prayer gathering), mention at least one of the convictions related to the event's purpose. If it's a long event (like a class), teach through all the convictions.

» In your pre-field training for short-term trips, make the very first session an overview of the convictions.

» If you have a missions wall or display, post your convictions for the entire church to see. Make copies available for members to take.

» If possible, do a sermon series based on your convictions (that is, preach from the passages that inform each conviction).

» When you have initial conversations with members who are interested in missions, share the convictions with them (or at least a few of them) over coffee or lunch.

» Teach an Introduction to Missions class. Make it a goal for every member to go through this class.

» Add your global missions vision to your new members class.

Teaching Vision

As we mentioned in Chapter 3, a sending vision is a short, clear, and memorable statement that answers the question, "Why do we exist?" Unlike the missions convictions, the vision can easily be on your lips at all times. In fact, you want it to be on *your* lips so much that it ends up on *others'* lips. This is like the net you use to constantly draw in all your missions hype and activity. It regularly reminds members why they're excited and what to do with it. Here are a few ways you can consistently teach vision:

» Say it—work it into every missions conversation. It may feel redundant or annoying, but the focus and clarity it brings are worth it. How can the entire church get involved if you keep the vision to yourself?

» Display it—post it in a creative, compelling way. Make it the centerpiece of your missions wall and displays. Use it on the homepage of your website. Get it tattooed on your forearm. (Just kidding—don't do that.)

» Draw it—be able to illustrate it on a napkin as you explain it. If possible, use symbols that help communicate it. This comes in handy in conversations over coffee. At the end, give them the napkin or have them take a picture of it.

» Pair it—anytime you teach your missions convictions, certainly, teach your vision as well. Show how the missions convictions lead into your vision.

» Highlight it—use it as the introduction to any missions events or trainings you do. Unlike the missions convictions, you can cover the vision in a much shorter amount of time. Even encourage your lead pastor to mention the vision when preaching about missions.

Teaching Strategy

As we mentioned in Chapter 4, a sending strategy answers the question, "How do we accomplish the vision?" It establishes guidelines that will help the church identify specific people, places, and/or projects in which they invest. This moves your church from the theoretical to the practical. Even though it is the work you constantly attend to, many members of the church will not naturally be interested in such details. Sometimes it will come up reactively because people will ask you to engage in a model and/or location that falls outside your strategy. But how can you teach it proactively? Consider these ways:

> » Just like you've worked to show how your missions convictions flow into your vision, show how your vision flows into your strategy. Again, symbols are helpful. A well-made infographic can really do the trick.
> » Make a short video that displays how your strategy works itself out in real life. Capture imagery from the locations where you engage. If possible, show scenes of the work taking place in those locations.
> » Utilize your missionaries to teach the strategy. They are living it out, so as they share about their ministry, tell them to frame it in the context of the strategy. This practice also serves to remind them that they're committed to the strategy.
> » When you report to pastors, staff, and the wider church body, communicate what's happening in terms of how the strategy is being fulfilled. Explain practical ways that the strategy depends on them.
> » Design your "on-ramps" to missions according to the strategy. For example, tie your prayer gatherings to your strategic locations, and explain why you're highlighting those locations.

Making the effort to consistently teach through your missions convictions, vision, and strategy may seem like daunting work. But most of the time when leaders get into the rhythms of it, they find it exhilarating. This isn't just because they experience the fun of seeing members "get it"; it's also because it constantly drives the convictions, vision, and strategy deeper into their own hearts. And that is joyful and contagious.

The intended result of this teaching, then, is that every member understands their roles and opportunities to participate in God's mission through the church. In other words, our goal is not that church members say, "Oh, look at what *those people* in our church do!" That's a missions ministry. The goal is that every member says, "Oh, this is how *I'm* part of what our church does!"

So, how does *that* happen?

The Sending Pipeline

One concept we'll frequently discuss in the coming chapters is a "sending pipeline." A sending pipeline is your process for identifying (Chapter 7), assessing (Chapter 8), and developing (Chapter 9) missionaries. Why introduce it here? And isn't a sending pipeline for a select group of people?

Although most church members will never pass through the body of the pipeline (identification, assessment, and development), all members should find themselves at the top opening of the pipeline. That means two different things.

First, every member has potential. Every church member should be challenged regularly to consider if God is calling them to be sent as a missionary. This applies to short-, mid-, and long-term commitments. It also applies to traditional and alternative paths (such as marketplace, business as missions, study abroad, retirement abroad, intentional tourism, military assignment, etc.). As members (including leaders) grow in their love for Jesus and his mission, it's healthy for them to be encouraged toward a posture of willingness, of offering God their lives as a blank check. You never know who might sense the inclination to be sent and who might become a fantastic missionary.

Second, every member is sent. Having every church member at the mouth of the sending pipeline means having every member thinking and acting like a missionary. This phrase was one of Upstream's early taglines. Our first book, *Tradecraft*, reflects this idea well. It teaches nine basic missionary skills for the everyday Christian. Why? So that every Christian can think and act like a missionary (even though they are not vocational missionaries). In the context of everyday life, they know how to follow the Spirit, build relationships, find persons of peace, contextualize, etc. And because of globalization, that means they even have the opportunity to engage cross-culturally among their neighbors from other nations. In order to foster this, church leaders can integrate every member's basic discipleship with sending theology and practice. Again, this is cultivating their sent identity.

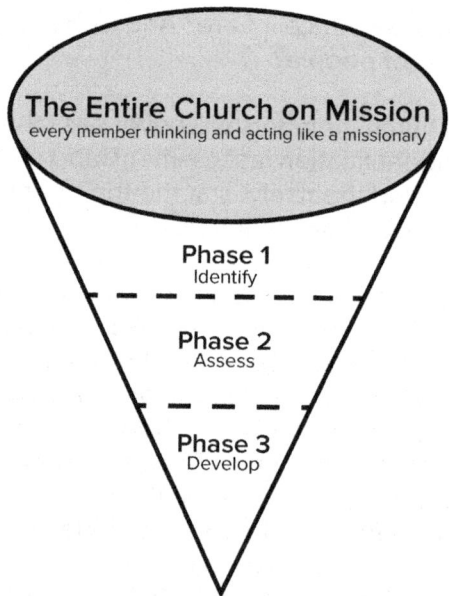

When every member thinks and acts like a missionary, then they are already thinking, "Oh, this is how *I'm* part of what our church does!" It's not a stretch, then, for them to relate to the vision of sending cross-culturally (especially if the language of local and global sending is similar). In fact, it could well be the basis for them getting excited about the work of your missionaries. If they can relate to and be excited about it, they will much more likely want to be part of it. At that point, the key is to ensure their roles and opportunities are clear. Here are some ways you might do that.

Focus on a particular passage of Scripture to catalyze every member's involvement in global sending. One such passage is 3 John 1:5–8, which says,

> "Beloved, it is a faithful thing you do in all your efforts for these brothers, strangers as they are, who testified to your love before the church. You will do well to send them on their journey *in a manner worthy of God*. For they have gone out for the sake of the name, accepting nothing from the Gentiles. *Therefore we ought to support people like these, that we may be fellow workers for the truth*" (emphasis mine).

This verse captures the idea of everyday Christians being co-laborers with missionaries in places they probably will never go. It also gives the sense of sending them as if they were sending Jesus himself ("in a manner worthy of God"). What a compelling vision!

Work with your leadership to develop church-wide opportunities for involvement. Think of this as low-hanging fruit. Although optional missions events can be helpful (such as prayer gatherings, missions conferences, and classes), what can you do in the regular church-wide rhythms of the congregation? For example, a quarterly "Sending Sunday" could ultimately be more impactful than an annual missions conference. Also, sending weekly prayer requests from your missionaries to your small groups could be more impactful than hosting a single prayer gathering.

Whenever you offer low-hanging-fruit opportunities, always

conclude with a pathway for reaching higher, for taking the next step. This might sound like, "As you pray regularly for our missionaries, we would like to invite you to join one of our advocate teams who are involved in the day-to-day care of our missionaries" (see Chapter 12, "Providing Ongoing Care"). Of course, not everyone will accept the invitation, but they will at least be aware of the opportunity.

Delineate what exactly are the sending roles of every member. One of the most common ways churches do this is by utilizing the phrase, "pray, give, go" (pray for missions, give to missions, and consider going on mission). A similar option could be "pray, give, care" (that is, be involved in the ongoing care of missionaries). Once you've captured a memorable phrase, specify what exactly you mean by each part. For example, you might say "we pray for our missionaries and their people groups in our homes, small groups, and worship services."

Once you have clarified and specified the sending roles of each member, take every opportunity to remind them of their roles. For example, when you commission a missionary, announce not only the missionary's roles toward the church but also the church's roles toward the missionary. Another example is prefacing any sending-related prayer with something like, "One of our commitments as church members is to pray regularly for our missionaries ..."

As you develop these opportunities, you will likely find that more members begin taking steps into the body of the sending pipeline. It's the natural result of being intimately involved in sending well. And that's exactly what you want to happen! For a more a detailed introduction to the sending pipeline, see the Appendix's "Developing a Sending Pipeline."

Developing a Sending Team

We understand that what we've discussed so far can represent a tremendous amount of work to launch, maintain, and grow.

That's why the last critical step toward involving the entire church is developing a sending team. This team is an infrastructure of missions leaders who help execute the sending process.

Why take the time to develop a sending team? The simple answer is so you don't have to do everything yourself! Trying to do everything yourself is not only counterproductive to the idea of involving the entire church, but it also presumes that you are omnicompetent. No one can do it all, and no one needs to try.

»» The Who ««

Consider the idea of the "Missions Pastor Profile" developed by Catalyst Services.[2] It enumerates the different "types" of missions leaders so they can understand their leadership style and build a sending team with complementary members. These styles include:

1. The Strategic Visionary: This missions leader develops visionary plans but is often drained by the details.
2. The Administrator: This type of missions leader builds on already developed plans and strategies and executes them excellently, but can often struggle with creating excitement.
3. The Missionary's Pastor: This type of missions leader loves to focus on the care of missionaries. While being great shepherds, they may lack the ability to develop a strategy.
4. The Mentor/Mobilizer: This type of missions leader loves to help members become effective in their global outreach. However, as they build relationships with missionaries, making difficult decisions can be hard for them.
5. The Field Leader/Partnership Developer: This type of missions leader's heart is on the front lines. In their efforts they make a great impact on the work of missions, but they can struggle to mobilize the hearts of members to that work.

Which type(s) are you? How can you maximize your strengths and gather a team around you to support your weaknesses? There is great freedom in self-awareness and leaning on the body of

Christ. Taking these steps is important in determining who your team will be.

»» The What ««

Alongside developing the "who" of your team is determining the "what" of your team. What roles do you need your team members to fill? There are many different ways that sending churches can assign roles within their sending team. Here are a few categorical examples:

Duration of Sending

This approach divides roles according to short-term sending (usually one week to two months), mid-term sending (usually between three months and three years), and long-term sending (usually a career commitment). Although there is much overlap between these categories, each one requires unique attention, especially logistically. Thus, one or more team members are devoted to executing a particular duration well. The strength of this model is that it provides multiple unique on-ramps for people to be sent. The weakness is that the sending team members can easily get siloed from one another rather than working as a cohesive unit.

Stage of Sending

This approach divides roles according to the long-term missionary's stages of pre-field, on-field, and post-field. It's easy for sending churches to thrive at one or two of these stages while neglecting the other(s). The most commonly neglected stage is post-field (see Chapter 15, "Receiving Sent Ones during Reentry"). The strength of this model is that the sending team is giving holistic attention to the life and work of long-term missionaries. The weakness is that it may lack relational continuity, meaning a missionary would always look to different leaders in different stages, limiting the depth of relationships over time.

Phase of Sending

This approach divides roles according to the phases of the sending pipeline: identification, assessment, and development. One or more leaders would be dedicated to recruiting and mobilizing members, one or more would be focused on interviewing and evaluating candidates, and one or more would be committed to preparing and training candidates. The strength of this model is that it can provide laser focus and excellence in raising up and sending out missionaries. The weakness is that it's focused entirely on the pre-field stage of sending.

Support of Sending

This approach divides roles according to specific elements of support: moral, logistical, financial, prayer, communication, and reentry. Missions leader Neal Pirolo unpacks these in his book *Serving as Senders Today*.[3] The strength of this model is that it gives leaders very specific categories to oversee, thus providing more comprehensive missionary care. The weakness, however, is that it leverages the sending team only toward the support of existing missionaries rather than raising up new ones.

Location of Sending

This approach divides roles according to the locations in which your church is engaging. That could mean the geographic ministries of local, domestic, and global (if the sending team is responsible for overseeing all of that) or the geographic categories of certain global regions, cities, or people groups. The strength of this model is that it broadens the scope of impact the sending team can have. At the same time, the weakness can be that the team is stretched very thin (or else it must be a really large team!).

Although each of these models has merit, what is often the most effective use of sending teams is a "tapestry" of roles based on

(1) what you need to fulfill your vision and strategy and (2) what human resources you have in and around your church. These roles could include (but are not limited to):

» Prayer leader: Helps mobilize prayer for missionaries and the nations

» Financial administrator: Helps with budgeting, book-keeping, and support-raising

» Communications leader: Helps with social media, marketing, and security

» Care advocate: Helps mobilize church members for missionary care

» Mobilizer: Helps recruit people into the sending pipe-line (identification)

» Trainer/Coach: Helps execute the sending process (development)

» Short-term trips leader: Helps plan and execute short-term mission trips

» Local missions: Helps mobilize members among internationals and refugees (see the Appendix for a resource on "Developing an International Ministry")

» Events coordinator: Helps plan and execute missions events

» Strategist: Helps build and maintain strategic focus (see Chapter 13, "Maintaining Strategic Focus")

» Pastor: Helps with spiritual oversight and connection to church leadership

This may already be obvious, but what we're saying is that a sending team should *not* be a committee that only allocates finances. Sending means much more than sending money. If you've inherited a sending team that operates that way, it will take time and wisdom to turn the tide. Introduce them to sending theology and vision. Consider reading through *The Sending Church Defined* together.[4] Involve them in the process of applying the Sending Church Elements (see Chapter 2, "Establishing Missions Convictions"). Above all, pray for their growth and excitement. And to dive deeper into building your sending team, the Appendix can direct you to a resource titled "Missions Leadership Team Development."

Joining the Movement

We introduced this chapter with the biblical example of Ephesus and how that entire church was involved in the mission. Because the entire church was involved, the fruit of their labor was exponential. One scholar argues that this movement alone gave birth to the churches at Smyrna, Pergamum, Thyatira, Sardis, Philadelphia, Laodicea, and likely many others.[5] Now *that* is a compelling cloud of witnesses!

Imagine how the fruit of your labor as a missions leader could be multiplied if everyone in the church participated. Consider the exponential impact of establishing a slow-brew sending culture, consistently teaching your missions convictions and practices, including everyone in your sending pipeline, and building a passionate sending team. It could be yet another significant movement in the history of Christianity.

—————————————————————————➤

PART 2: DEVELOPMENT PHASE

The church prepares its own members to be sent.

Chapters 1 to 5 covered the Sending Church Elements in the "Establishing" phase. There, you learned how to lay a healthy foundation for sending by creating awareness, establishing missions convictions, developing vision, building strategy, and involving all church members.

Now we must consider how all that effort can begin to directly impact the nations. We call Sending Church Elements #6 to #9 the "Developing" phase. This is where you begin to develop missionaries. The next few chapters will help you find the right partnerships, identify those that could be sent, assess them, and develop them for sending cross-culturally.

◀—————————————————————————

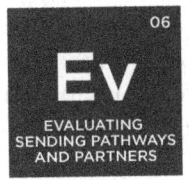

SENDING CHURCH ELEMENT #6:
EVALUATING SENDING PATHWAYS & PARTNERS

by Mike Easton

> *A sending church proactively evaluates sending pathways and partners that align with its convictions, vision, and strategy for the purpose of finding the most fitting global partners and missions organizations. These entities not only help facilitate sending but also align theologically, remain relationally accessible, and uphold the centrality of the local church.*

As a college pastor, I had the privilege of regularly meeting with young men to disciple and mentor them. While we always had conversations about their life with God and their ministry to the campus, our conversations would inevitably turn to life's big decisions: "Am I in the right major?" "Should I be taking on this much debt?" "What kind of job should I get after college?" "I like this girl. Should I date her?" "I really like this girl. Should I marry her?"

College and young professional years are such a formational time. The decisions young people make during these years will impact the rest of their lives. Think of yourself in the journey of this book as though you are in that college/young professional stage. You've chosen your "major" or "apprenticeship" by developing your vision and strategy. As you journey towards the end of this formational season, you are thinking about what you really want to do and who you want to do that with as a church.

In this chapter, we will look at evaluating sending pathways and partners. The sending pathway, to continue with the college/young professional analogy, is choosing your career path. It is the avenue by which you will enter a location with sustainability and bring value to the people who live there. The partnership is choosing who you will work with and who you will work for.

We will guide you in evaluating the right sending pathway for gaining access to the people you want to reach. We will also evaluate partners such as the sending organization, the on-field team, and the indigenous leaders. Evaluating the entry pathway and ministry partners is foundational to sending well, as both will have a tremendous impact on the missionary's flourishing and ultimately the success of the mission God has given to your church.

Part 1: Evaluating Sending Pathways

A sending pathway is the mode by which the missionary will enter the country in a viable way, provide value to the community, and minister to the people with whom they will engage. This is often referred to as a missionary's "platform." It is how the missionary relevantly answers the questions "Why are you here?" and "What value do you bring?" A pathway might include (but is not limited to) being a vocational missionary, studying a language, teaching English, transferring jobs through a multinational company, providing humanitarian aid or healthcare, starting a new business, or residing as a retiree or remote worker.

There are five values that sending churches and their missionaries can consider to evaluate the effectiveness of a sending pathway.

These values include the missionary's

1. Accessibility - Effectively gains access to the people
2. Flexibility - Allows capacity for engaging with people
3. Sustainability - Provides ongoing finances
4. Credibility - Brings value to the community
5. Geography - Puts them in direct contact with their people

Now let's unpack these values one at a time.

Accessibility

A sending pathway needs to provide access to the people with whom the missionary wants to engage. Without proximity, it is difficult for real ministry to take place. If the missionary cannot enter and stay in the country for a sustained period of time, or if the pathway does not provide regular, face-to-face access to the people to whom they are ministering, then it is not a viable option. Some questions to consider for accessibility include:

» Will the missionary have direct access to the people we want to engage?
» Can the missionary get a visa to live in the location long-term?

Flexibility

While a sending pathway may provide accessibility to people, churches must also ask if the missionary will have the time required to do ministry with their target group. For example, those taking a job, creating a business, or enrolling in a university may be able to get a visa, but will they have a flexible enough schedule to learn some language and culture and minister to the people? Some questions to consider for flexibility include:

» How many hours is the missionary expected to work

per week?

» Are the hours flexible enough for fulfilling their other responsibilities and building relationships?

Sustainability

If a particular sending pathway has been chosen, churches must determine how long it will be sustainable. For example, taking a job or creating a business may be a good pathway for bringing viability to the missionary and value to the community, but the pace of life it requires or the finances it provides may not be sustainable. The new missionary may need to raise support both to provide flexibility in their schedule and to make up for the lower income that results from not working full-time.

Those raising full-time support must consider if what they raise will cover their family's and ministry's growing needs. Some sending churches and missionaries also have particular convictions regarding the amount of support they will raise (i.e., whether they are seeking full support, partial support, or being fully funded by a missions organization or job). These need to be considered when deciding what sending pathway to pursue. Some questions to ask when considering sustainability include:

» What is the financial goal of the missionary? Is it to raise full-time or part-time support? Do they hope to be fully funded through a job or business?

» Does the sending pathway provide a sustainable way for the missionary to live in that country?

Credibility

Credibility determines whether the sending pathway brings value to the community to whom the missionary is ministering. As we mentioned above, one of the most common questions a missionary will receive from locals is, "What do you do for work?" Working is an aspect of being an image-bearer. Work existed before the fall (Genesis 1:26–28), and it is important to both the believer and the unbeliever to work and bring value to the community.

In Mandarin there is an important word that is hard to translate into English: "guanxi." The word encapsulates the idea of value and relational trust. If one has "guanxi" with someone in China, they have shown that they bring value to a person or community, are trustworthy, and have gained relational credibility. "Guanxi," in any context, is vital for the incarnational ministry of the gospel. A credible sending pathway aids the development of "guanxi."

These sending pathways need to be carefully thought through in each context. Whether the pathway is starting a coffee shop, a medical mission, learning language, or working for a transnational company, the sending pathway needs to provide the missionary with credibility amongst the people with whom they are working.

Here are some questions to consider for credibility:

> » What value will the missionary bring to the community through their sending pathway?
> » Does the sending pathway—and the work done within it—make sense to the people who live there?

Geography

While accessibility, flexibility, sustainability, and credibility are important for a sending pathway, they mean nothing if the missionary can't go the last few feet to talk face to face with their target people. For example, engaging unreached people groups can mean living in extreme circumstances, which can create a barrier to sustainable living for some families.

Many missionaries will choose to live outside of their target people group for teaming, children's education, and access to resources.

Without the correct sending pathway in place, these choices can lead to long commutes and extended periods of time away from home. If living at a geographical distance is the only sustainable option, then the missionary and sending church must carefully consider whether that location is the most strategic. Questions to consider regarding geography include:

> » Will the missionary be able to live and work near the people they are engaging? If not, will they be able to commute easily and regularly to the people?
> » Are there near-culture people(s) who would better fit the viable sending pathway to those people?

Sending Pathways

Now that we have established the values a missionary and sending church need to think through when considering pathways, here are three broad pathway categories (please note, these are not the only pathways, just the most common): vocational missions, marketplace missions, and business as missions. Let's give consideration to each one.

Vocational Missions

Vocational missions is typically for those who focus the majority of their time and energy directly on evangelism, discipling indigenous believers, and multiplying the work of the gospel in an area of the world. This is most viable in settings where, for example, religious visas are available, language learning is a possible route to receive a visa, retirees are allowed to live on an extended visa that does not require a job, or where it makes sense for foreigners to have a different daily routine than locals. The benefit is that this pathway allows the missionaries to focus the majority of their efforts on whatever they deem most strategic.

However, vocational missions may not be as viable in areas

where where, for example, there is government persecution against Christianity, visas are not easy to obtain, or the value of the missionary in the community is questioned. This is often the case in the unreached and unengaged areas of the world. Rarely will a cross-cultural missionary in an unreached or unengaged area of the world utilize the vocational missions route without implementing an alternative pathway such as studying language, teaching English, or relying on another platform for getting into and remaining in that area.

Marketplace Missions

This pathway is for those who move cross-culturally because of, for example, a job with a multinational company, an opportunity with an organization or institution, or the freedom of remote work. They then accomplish ministry in the workplace and during their non-work time in the community.

Marketplace missions can be a great path for cross-cultural ministry. Much of the gospel movement in the world has been accomplished by those who used their vocation to build relationships, model the Christian life, and speak the gospel. Since most new believers will not go into full-time ministry, this pathway also offers a reproducible way to train new disciples to be on mission wherever they are. It also provides natural life-on-life opportunities with people that a vocational missions route would lack.

Marketplace ministry is not without its challenges. It can be difficult to do ministry, learn a language, and work a job simultaneously. Because of the importance of contextualization, it is ideal for cross-cultural workers pursuing this pathway to give a dedicated season to learning language and culture. However, this is rarely possible due to the demands of transitioning overseas and employers' expectations for productivity.

Some marketplace missionaries will seek local, part-time opportunities that provide a visa and a valuable way to be in the country, while not requiring forty hours of work per week. These roles can often provide real value to the community (though we should be aware of the possibility and perception of taking jobs from locals), give space for ministry in the marketplace, and leave time for ministry beyond work. In these scenarios the worker generally has to raise support to cover the rest of their costs.

Another viable and increasing sending pathway is that of the "digital nomad." In our age of remote work, many people are able to work from anywhere in the world and have great flexibility. For those with an adventurous spirit and a love for their work, being a digital nomad can provide a great means for living and doing ministry among their target people. The missionary pursuing this pathway needs to consider how the change in time zones will impact their life rhythms and how they will creatively place themselves among locals, especially if they will be working primarily from home.

Another consideration for marketplace workers is how they will interact with a local church or existing missions team. For example, if the vision is for them to plant a church, will they have time to work toward that in addition to fulfilling their job responsibilities? This is beyond the capacity of many marketplace workers, which is why we would recommend a formal or informal connection with a missions team or local church, both for community and for the development of the local body of believers.

If your church embraces the vision of sending marketplace missionaries, have a plan for how you will help them get connected and on mission wherever they move. Give them a vision for utilizing their work opportunity for kingdom purposes. Take advantage of resources like Upstream's global marketplace training and Larry McCrary's book *The MarketSpace: Essential Relationships Between the Sending Church, Marketplace Worker, and Missionary Team.*

While marketplace missions is challenging, it is becoming one of the more viable and necessary pathways for sending. Visas are becoming increasingly difficult to obtain as countries grow more hostile to missionary work and better equipped to identify it. This path doesn't fit neatly into a box, so the sending church and marketplace worker pursuing it will need patience, perseverance, and a tolerance for trial and error.

Business as Mission

This pathway is for those who move cross-culturally and start a business. Their business may simply be a means of providing for their own living and ministry expenses, but, ideally, it will also support the employment of locals who will be able to hear and see the gospel lived out by the missionaries they work with. This pathway may also be called "Business for Transformation."

When done well, Business as Mission can be one of the most effective ways to enter into an unreached and, especially, unengaged culture. The creation of a business that provides value to a local community can help the cross-cultural worker gain credibility with those they are trying to reach. Also, providing jobs for indigenous people can bring particular value to the world's developing areas. Long term, a well-run business can provide the flexibility for the cross-cultural worker to engage in ministry beyond the workplace.

To be able to create a business in another culture, it is valuable to have created a business in one's own culture. Often the worker will have to take the time to learn the local language—possibly even two languages—to be an effective business person. And both the worker and their sending church must remember that creating a business and then developing it to lead to gospel impact can take a great deal of time. It takes an especially patient and entrepreneurial missionary to adopt this approach and stick with it. It also takes a patient sending church. However, in the hardest-to-reach regions of the world, this route may be the most viable pathway and is, therefore, worth the time and effort it requires.

Part 2: Evaluating Missions Organizations

Missions organizations serve as a bridge between sending pathways and on-field partnerships. Each person will have differing needs for a missions organization depending on their overseas experience, their support-raising requirements, and the particular pathway by which they will enter the field of ministry.

In most cases, partnering with a missions organization to accomplish your vision for your missionary and church will be an important aspect of your sending strategy. In the next section, we will look at how to determine your on-field partnerships, but before we do, we need to consider the umbrella that covers most on-field partnerships: the missions organization.

The missions organization often shapes the on-field partners through its employment policies, training, and culture. While on-field partners will ultimately determine the culture of their team, any overarching employment structure will shape those who work underneath it. As you get to know on-field partners, it is important to consider what role the organization plays in the day-to-day life of that partner.

In the modern missions movement, missions organizations started as "societies," often within denominations, to gather funding for missionaries. As these missions societies developed, they grew to provide an increasing number of services, like fundraising training and gift processing; accounting services, human resources, and legal frameworks; and oversight from afar, mostly through letters.

As societies developed and matured their sending processes, they added more practices and systems. These included identification of missionaries, pre-field training, on-the-ground oversight, a specified vision and strategy, and care for missionaries.

Missions organizations have accomplished incredible things for the kingdom of God. As they have grown, however, churches have become increasingly dependent on them to take care of their people and have outsourced much of the work of missions, work which we believe is the responsibility of the sending church. This shift in responsibility was understandable. Before the technological advances and globalization that took place in the late twentieth and the early twenty-first centuries, many local churches were at a loss on how to send and care for missionaries who served in faraway places. As a result, missions organizations continued to take on more and more of the sending process.

Thanks to modern travel, telecommunications, and the rise in short-term trips, it has become increasingly feasible for sending churches to reclaim aspects of sending that were their responsibility all along. But while this desire has increased among sending churches, it has taken time for sending churches and missions organizations to work through what partnership in sending should be. Therefore, as your church works alongside sending organizations, it is important that you understand the respective roles each entity will play in sending and caring for those you send. For most sending churches, it is not wise to forgo partnership with a missions organization.

I've been a missionary, a missions pastor, a consultant to sending churches, and a leader in a missions organization. I have been the partner on the field, the one searching for partners, and part of the organization that's trying to maximize the impact of all these entities for the benefit of the missionary. Through these roles I've learned that strong connections between the sending church, the missions organization, and field partners exponentially improve the experience and increase the longevity of the missionary, both of which lead to greater fruitfulness on the field.

How do you determine what to look for in a missions organization for your missionaries? As a church that values sending, look for organizations that value the sending church's role in assessing, developing, and caring for missionaries. Look for organizations that not only fit your vision and strategy but that also see the centrality of the local church in sending. Look for organizations that do not simply say this with their words and slogans but that also integrate it into their systems and strategies. To help you with this, see the Appendix, which can direct you to a list of "Questions for Evaluating Missions Organizations."

Part 3: Evaluating Sending Partners

While evaluating the missions organization is important, who your missionaries will be led by and work with daily is just as important. Many of us have had a job that we liked but that was with the wrong people. Being in the right job with the wrong boss or co-workers is a miserable experience. If a particular supervisor or the team's culture is problematic, then your missionary's life will likely be difficult.

The goal of having an on-field team leader is to provide vision and daily oversight of the missionary from your church. Your church's geographical and time-zone distance and your inability to understand the unique ministry within the local culture necessitate meaningful partnership with the team leader.

One of the most common reasons a missionary returns from the field is not the difficulty of living overseas, but issues with their team. Taking the time to evaluate the team leader's character, disposition, vision, successes/failures, theological convictions, practical leadership skills, missiology, methodology, care strategies, etc. will impact your missionary tremendously.

Missionary care is an important topic we will dive into in Chapter 12, Providing Ongoing Care. The care of missionaries is one of the most crucial roles of the sending church, and it can begin before they ever leave. You can care for them in this pre-field stage by helping them get on a team that shares your church's vision, values, and strategies, and that practices healthy rhythms of outward ministry and care for one another.

Discovering Healthy Teams

The good news is that there are a lot of great team leaders and teams overseas. So, how do you find the ones that will help your missionaries thrive? I've found a few things that are critical in finding healthy teams: time and experience, networking, trips, and prayer.

Time and Experience

If you have ever bought a house, then you've likely heard the advice "Don't buy the first house you see." You need to look at and compare four or five houses to help you discern what you like and what a certain size or type of house should cost.

As a missions leader, don't just choose the first team you see. Consider multiple teams, which will not only allow you to compare them, but also discern what you like and what you don't.

This process takes time and experience. It takes the sovereignty of God that cannot be rushed. Many teams will seem great at first glance, but before committing short-term, mid-term, or long-term church members to their leadership, you must take the time to truly understand that team's vision and culture. Patience is an important virtue in developing partnerships.

Networking

Because your role as a missions leader often takes you beyond the walls of your church, networking will be an important skill for you to develop. Ask your denomination, network, or affiliated missions organizations for referrals to great partnerships. Ask friends and co-laborers at other churches whom they are partnered with. Make a list of potential partners. Then run these potential partners through the "Partnership Matrix" exercise we outlined in Chapter 4.

Trips

As you begin to identify potential teams, take a trip to visit them. A few thousand dollars invested in a trip is a drop in the bucket compared to the hundreds of thousands of dollars that will be invested in a missionary over the years. There really is no substitute for an in-person assessment of a team. Video calls will only tell you so much. Getting to view firsthand the ministry they are doing, the team's culture, how they act when they are tired or stressed, and the viability of the strategy in that location is necessary for fully vetting a partnership.

Prayer

Last, but obviously not least, is prayer. In Acts 13:2, Luke tells us the members of the church of Antioch were "worshiping God and fasting," and it was in this context that God revealed his desire for them to send out Paul and Barnabas. Do not rush partnerships. Ask the Lord to guide you in his providence. There is no formula to follow for hearing God's call on your church and your people, but gathering in corporate prayer to seek God's will should be a prerequisite to all we do for the Lord.

And as you do that, the Appendix can direct you to an extensive list of "Questions for Evaluating On-Field Partners." God has raised up wonderful laborers in his harvest. Go find them!

Part 4: Partnering with Indigenous Believers

Finally, let's take a look at partnering with indigenous believers. This is an area of important consideration because God's global mission is carried out through his global church. Unfortunately, Western missions practice has sometimes been characterized as domineering, neglecting the value of indigenous believers. In reality, these believers often can carry out the work more effectively, which doesn't remove the need for missionaries, but invites them (and the churches who send them) to take more supportive roles. Just as we see in the church at Antioch, multiethnic mission is a powerful expression of the kingdom of God.

Missions leader Ellen Livingood gives five important points to consider for partnering well with indigenous believers.[1] They are:

1. Doctrinal Compatibility - As in any partnership, you must decide if the work is compatible with your theology. In indigenous partnerships, be generous in areas that are not crucial or that may be expressed differently because of language or culture.
2. Existing Vision and Leadership - A mistake that well-intentioned Western groups tend to make is to assert their ideas on partners. Instead, ask them what they want and only come alongside the ideas they produce.
3. Reciprocity - While the indigenous partner has needs, remember that they are image bearers full of the Holy Spirit. While we might provide a need in an area, it's important to look humbly at how they can serve you and your church through the partnership.
4. Look beyond the Initial Option - Get to know some partners before fully diving into a partnership with one. Getting to know different partners will help you get a sense of what you desire in an indigenous partner and will help you make a better decision.
5. Focus on Relationships, Not Projects - As Westerners we often see material needs before relational needs. Look first for relationships that you want to build over projects you want to complete.

We also recommend looking for indigenous partners who are accountable to others, whether it's an existing organization or a plurality of leadership. It's important to have accountability in place and good references for that person. Partnering with indigenous believers can be tricky. Our assumptions about leadership, and sometimes even morality, may not be shared across cultural lines, so we need to partner wisely, especially when funding is involved.

As in all partnerships, you won't get it right 100 percent of the time. Partnering is more art than science. In order to help you discern potential indigenous partners, consider using some of the "Questions for Evaluating Missions On-Field Partners" as listed in the Appendix.

Finding Incredible People

Looking back on my days as a college pastor, I'm thankful for the young men who took time to seek out the wisdom of someone older than them. How joyful it has been to watch the marriages, the careers, and the gospel impact of these young men. Had they rushed the decisions about their major, career, or spouse, I wonder how different their lives may have looked.

As I also look back on partnerships my church made with on-field team leaders, I'm thankful for the way God led our church to connect with the right missions organizations and the right on-field partners. Not every partnership worked out forever, but in his sovereignty, God led us to incredible people doing incredible work among the nations. I am confident he will do that for you as well. Following the processes outlined in this chapter can't guarantee you'll always partner with the right people, but I pray that some of what we've suggested here, combined with the work of the Holy Spirit, will lead you to fruitful partnerships that will impact eternity.

SENDING CHURCH ELEMENT #7: IDENTIFYING MISSIONARIES

By Larry McCrary

> *A sending church identifies missionaries by deliberately calling members to take the next step of obedience in God's mission. Instead of waiting for volunteers, church leaders mobilize the congregation by affirming and challenging those with the potential to be sent cross-culturally. Candidates are thus called to intentionally enter the next phase of the sending pipeline.*

What do you do with someone in your church who senses God may be leading them to the mission field?

Joe and Wendy have been married for ten years. Joe listens to a popular mission speaker at an online conference and starts following him on social media. Then, he follows all of the people the speaker follows. Pretty soon he is inundated with opportunities and the idea that everyone should go to the nations. There is a specific country that keeps coming to his mind. He talks to his wife about it, but compared to her, he is further down the road in this conversation. She has not thought about it as much, nor is she as interested.

They are both mature followers of Jesus and are actively involved in their church. They attend regularly, give consistently, and serve on various ministry teams. They even lead a small group and have proven to possess good leadership and shepherding skills.

The pastor of the church is preaching through the Book of Acts, and there have been multiple opportunities for them to respond to his message. You are the missions leader and have been able to take advantage of the sermon series and its effect on church members. This past Sunday, your pastor asked if any member has an interest in serving overseas as a vocational missionary or marketplace missionary. Joe sends you a text and wants to meet over coffee.

Only Joe comes to the meeting. His wife does not make it. He starts telling you his story and how he feels God is specifically calling him to be a missionary to South Asia.

But clearly there is something wrong with this scenario. How could the sending church be helpful to Joe and Wendy in this situation?

Biblical Introduction

Sending churches should love the story of Paul and his young counterpart, Timothy. We can look into their ministry partnership at several points in the New Testament and draw out some significant principles in identifying potential missionaries.

We first read about Timothy in Acts 16:1–3:

> Paul came to Derbe and then to Lystra, where a disciple named Timothy lived, whose mother was Jewish and a believer but whose father was a Greek. The believers at Lystra and Iconium spoke

> well of him. Paul wanted to take him along on the journey, so he circumcised him because of the Jews who lived in that area, for they all knew that his father was a Greek.

It is beyond the scope of this conversation to talk about the last part of verse 3 and Timothy's circumcision. However, it is important to note here that the believers in Lystra and Iconium gave Timothy their recommendation. The local church knew Timothy. They likely had been discipling him and watching him grow. They had observed his life. Paul knew his family, and his mother was a believer. Paul must have sensed that Timothy was someone who had potential in ministry. Paul made it clear that he wanted Timothy to join his team, and the believers of Lystra and Iconium affirmed this step for Timothy.

When you pick up the story later in Paul's second letter to Timothy, you read that Paul confirmed the gift that had been obvious since Timothy joined the team. Paul confirmed his desire to have Timothy join his ministry and, at that point, minister in his own church. Paul writes in 2 Timothy 3:14, "But as for you, continue in what you have learned and have firmly believed, knowing from whom you learned it and how from childhood you have been acquainted with the sacred writings, which are able to make you wise for salvation through faith in Christ Jesus."

Timothy proved to be an asset to Paul's ministry. In the second chapter of Philippians, we read:

> I hope in the Lord Jesus to send Timothy to you soon, so that I too may be cheered by news of you. For I have no one like him, who will be genuinely concerned for your welfare. For they all seek their own interests, not those of Jesus Christ. But you know Timothy's proven worth, how as a son with a father he has served with me in the gospel. (Philippians 2:19–22)

In the same way, as local church leaders desiring to be good senders, we can observe the potential in people already serving and living out the gospel in a local church. Our churches are full of potential missionaries. Often, leaders need to take the first step and challenge potential missionaries to move forward in God's mission. Look for the potential, not the perfection. Disciple and develop these future missionaries.

Two Approaches to Identifying Missionaries: Reactive and Proactive

When identifying potential missionaries, there are two approaches we can take: reactive and proactive. While each is viable, we want to encourage you towards proactive identification of potential missionaries.

The Reactive Approach

I have worked with hundreds of churches over the years, and most do not have a system for identifying potential missionaries. Most only respond when a person comes to the pastor or missions leader and tells them of their potential calling. In many cases, the pastor does not even know about this person's interest until their missions organization asks them for an endorsement for the potential missionary. This is what I call a reactive approach. The church is simply reacting to the needs of the future missionaries.

The first step in improving upon this approach is to set up a simple process or pipeline to identify potential missionaries and respond to those who show interest. This will be helpful as you prepare future missionaries, and the missions organizations and the field teams will appreciate this preparedness.

There will undoubtedly be people in your church who are responding to God's calling through hearing speakers, podcasts, missions conferences, prayer, Bible studies, etc. They will come to you and ask for your help. With a good system, you can begin cultivating their calling to missions.

For many churches, this process begins with broad mission events or a mission emphasis on a Sunday morning to cultivate awareness. To start identifying potential missionaries, these churches will have a clear "next step" or "call to action" coming out of these events. Some will use a response card or online form for church members to complete. I have seen some churches host a follow-up event where interested church members can gather together and learn about taking the next step.

As missions leaders, we need to be ready to "react" to those interested in missions by having clear next steps for discerning their calling and obeying what God is leading them to do.

But what if there is a way to take a more proactive approach to identifying missionaries?

The Proactive Approach

A sending church must lay out a vision to send men and women to the nations. They will develop a strategy that will find multiple ways to engage people, places, or projects. They will no doubt recognize that a part of that strategy will be to send out their own members to other nations.

Acts 13, which we reference often in this book, provides a description of (not a prescription for) identifying potential missionaries. In Acts 13:1–3, the church leaders of Antioch were praying and fasting. The Holy Spirit told them to set apart Paul and Barnabas for the work they had been called to do. At this point, Paul and Barnabas had likely been with the church of Antioch for about six years (Acts 11–12). They were two of the five leaders in the church. The church was proactively praying and fasting—for what, we don't know. But they heard God and acted upon that call to send.

While God works through the reactive approach to identify missionaries, we would also like to encourage you to consider how you can become more proactive in your sending. There are a few key ways to be proactive: know what kind of person you want to send, identify the mobilization pools in your church, and train yourself and your staff to have ICNU ("I see in you") conversations. Let's take a look at each of these.

What Kind of Person Do You Want to Send?

A critical first step a church should take to identify missionaries proactively is to determine the key qualities a person should have as a missionary. If you know what type of person you are looking to send, you will be able to proactively discover, identify, and cultivate those people already in your church.

Here is a graphic we developed with a list of important qualities of potential missionaries:[1]

We will come back to this graphic in Chapter 8 as we dive into

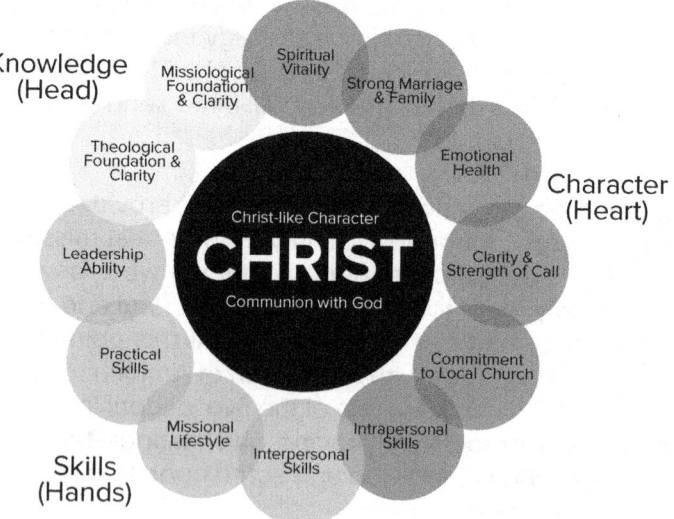

assessing the readiness of potential missionaries. At this stage, members you are identifying do not need to have all these qualities in full. There should, however, be identifiable seedlings of these qualities that can be nurtured and developed. A person should not be identified because of the hope of these characteristics but by a demonstration of them.

Missions organizations will do their best to evaluate these skills, but there is no one better able to identify and assess a potential missionary than their church leader who knows them well and observes their life and ministry. It is through intentional observation that we move from reactive to proactive identification of missionaries.

A missions leader cannot do this alone. You will need to train fellow staff members, elders, and lay leaders to identify potential missionaries. It's an important skill of a leader to be able to identify other leaders. I'm sure the leadership of your church is already doing this. Teach them how to take the next step to identify potential missionaries. Develop a culture of identification that not only identifies the next small group leader but also identifies the next missionary.

What Are Your Mobilization Pools?

Identifying mobilization pools in our churches starts with what we observe in members' church involvement—not merely their attendance, but their active involvement in and service to the church. They may be in leadership roles, or they may be that faithful servant in a variety of different areas. They may be bent towards serving in the city with your church ministries or other local non-profit ministries.

As you observe their lives, take notice of their posture. Are they a learner? Humble? Flexible? Adaptable? Do they share the gospel? Are they disciple-makers?

These are not missions-specific qualities but qualities you would look for in selecting someone to invest your time into as a leader. Begin investing in these people as they live missionally through the life and programs of your church. If they begin to show particular entrepreneurial gifting, the ability to go through really hard things, and a growing desire and ability to share the gospel, you'll know they're the right type of person to increase your investment in.

What Are the ICNU Conversations?

I first learned about "ICNU conversations" from a church in Fort Wayne, Indiana. These are conversations that begin with "I see in you ..." The missions pastor there told me that as he observes members serving in their church in various areas, he makes it a point to challenge people to go to the nations. He will tell them things like:

>> "I see in you a servant spirit among refugees in our city."
>> "I see that you are always talking about sharing the gospel wherever you work, live, or play."
>> "Have you ever considered taking a job overseas?"
>> "Have you ever considered becoming a cross-cultural missionary?"

He does not wait for them to come to him at a missions event, though he welcomes that opportunity. He also proactively asks people to consider cross-cultural missions.

Other Examples

Several years ago, when I was back in the States partnering with a church, we began a monthly missions chat where we invited anyone in the church interested in going to the nations. We shared a meal together. We prayed for our missionaries and their ministries. We chose a topic each month to discuss life overseas. It was an entry-level event where we could start the conversation about missions. Over the course of the following month, we connected with the people who attended to have coffee, pray, and continue to explore the idea of going on mission.

Some churches encourage members who have shown interest or have been identified as potential missionaries to be a part of the international outreach ministry for at least a year before considering going overseas. Adding this step helps the missions leaders get around potential missionaries to see if they have the characteristics and the competencies to go cross-culturally as they start down the path of determining if this is a calling God has on their life.

Calling

David Frazier writes, "Part of the missionary attrition today ... is caused by a misunderstanding or doubt regarding calling. Thus many who believe they were called into overseas ministry end up struggling with doubt and confusion once on the field."[2] Once you have identified a potential missionary in your church, or they have made themselves known, what is the next step?

In Chapter 8 we will talk in depth about assessment. At this point in the process, however, walking the potential missionary through a basic exercise in calling can be helpful. We do not want to assume that everyone who shows interest in going overseas automatically should. As we have shared, a potential missionary should demonstrate particular qualities prior to being launched overseas. So, how do we help them determine and affirm their calling?

First, we must recognize that calling happens both internally and externally. The potential missionary needs to have a clear sense that the work of a missionary is what they are supposed to do. As we have mentioned, this internal calling needs to be affirmed, or even predicated, by the local church (i.e., externally).

While calling is important during this discerning stage prior to going overseas, it becomes especially important when on the field. In the dark days and seasons of language learning, making cultural blunders, and wishing for what was at home, returning to one's internal calling affirmed by the church's external calling can be an anchor that keeps a missionary on the field.

Second, a wonderful grid for discerning calling is found in an article by the late Tim Keller titled "Vocation: Discerning Your Calling."[3] This article is helpful for discerning any type of calling, and I would recommend it for the college student who can't decide on their major, to the church member going through a midlife crisis, and to the person discerning if they should become a missionary.

Keller says that there is a primary and general calling that we all have as Christians to orient our lives around loving God and loving people (Matthew 22:37) and making him known around the world (Matthew 28:18–20). This is true for the engineer, the teacher, the student, the stay-at-home mom, and the missionary.

As all believers everywhere live to fulfill this calling, God provides each person a secondary calling regarding their vocation. It is through this vocation that God provides for the needs of the believer, but vocation is also an avenue for making Christ known.

As we have mentioned, living and ministering as a missionary is not the vocation for everyone. There are ways to make disciples of all nations in our own country and to be involved in praying for, mobilizing, and funding missionaries. Regardless of the path we take to do it, we all need to utilize our vocation and our time to make disciples of all nations. God will specifically call some believers to full-time, vocational missions. For those identified as potential missionaries, it is important to discern internally and externally if this is what the Lord truly desires for that person.

How do we discern this? Keller gives a helpful grid for discerning this secondary calling that can be utilized in the first stage of identifying missionaries. This Venn diagram of calling is composed of passion, ability, and context:

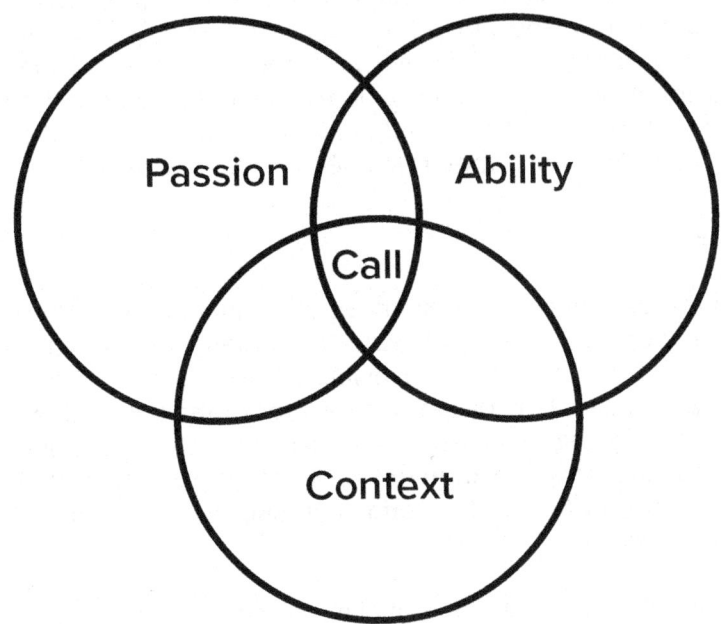

Passion

Does the potential missionary have a passion for the glory of God among the nations? Does that person gravitate towards those who are lost or those who are different from them? If they do, this is great affirmation that they are geared towards missionary work.

I often hear people say, "I see God's call in the Great Commission, but I just don't have a passion for it." At this point, I will sometimes substitute "affinity" for "passion" to take away the charged nature of the latter word. "Passion" can often be translated as "ecstatic," "excited," or "energetic." While passion may mean these words, it has more to do with whether something is important to you and causes you to orient your life around it.

If a potential missionary is struggling to discern if they have an affinity for taking the gospel to the nations, I encourage them to find ways to foster missions affinity. Whether it is by studying Scripture passages about God's love for all nations, reading a missionary biography, or spending time with someone from another country, it is vital for all believers to have a heartbeat for the nations. I would argue that these are important steps in the maturation of every believer in discerning their role in God's global vision.

Ability

Does the potential missionary have the right gift mix? Has he or she developed the right skill set for overseas life and ministry? At minimum, are they growing towards those abilities? There's no one-size-fits-all list of abilities and gifts for a missionary. However, some important abilities that someone ministering cross-culturally should demonstrate include grit/resilience, flexibility, a heart for evangelism, ability to walk through hardship, relational worth, and emotional maturity.

How do you discern if a potential missionary has these qualities and abilities? The most helpful way to discern this is through observation. Does what they do in the life of your church match up with what a missionary would do? How do they fare on a short-term trip or in the context of ministering to those who are different from them? Remember: past experience is a good predictor of future performance.

Have them take a spiritual gifts test and a few personality tests. While we never want these tests to become self-fulfilling prophecies for the person, they can be useful in putting some language to and working through a person's strengths and weaknesses.

Context

Does the cross-cultural context and opportunity line up with their life circumstances? If they have a lot of debt, aging parents, older kids, etc., cross-cultural ministry might not be the best context for them. Or they may have the right passion and ability for overseas work in general, but not specifically for a particular context. Need doesn't constitute calling. There will always be needs around the world. We should help our people discern the opportunity and the context that God is calling them to.

While we are all called to make disciples of all nations, I have seen far too many missionaries end up in a situation that did not fit them because they or their church did not take the time to assess their passion, ability, and the opportunity before them.

Improper Motivations

As we help members of our churches discern their calling towards missions, we need to cultivate the right motivations in them and watch for where they are improperly motivated. Here are six improper—but easily disguised—motivations.

Feeling Significant before God

Some believe that missions is the work and commitment that pleases God the most. After all, it is the most obvious way to obey the Great Commission. But becoming a full-time missionary will not fix problems in their personal, spiritual, or family lives. Significance must be found in Christ, not in the work they are doing. As soon as failure or lack of fulfillment comes, they will quickly look for other paths to finding their significance.

Pleasing Someone Else (Parents, Mentors, Etc.)

This improper motivation can easily be disguised, so you will need to observe a potential missionary's life to see if it exists. Many pursue missions because they want to please someone in their life who is encouraging them to consider cross-cultural ministry.

If what they say about missions around others is not what they practice in daily life, then it may be a sign that they aren't pursuing missions out of a personal calling, which means you should slow down the sending process with this person.

In some cases parents project their own missional desires onto their children, especially if the parents are involved in missions or ministry themselves. As you get to know your candidates, it will be important for them to be able to articulate their own missions motivations. Helping them cultivate a heart for missions from the Scriptures is the best way to ensure they are pursuing missions out of a sense of personal conviction and calling and not just to please those they look up to.

Impressing Others

Being a missionary is considered radical by many. People are often drawn to missions for this reason, and someone's ego can easily be uplifted by the praise they receive for going overseas. This idol often comes crashing down as they realize that missionary work is not as romantic as many believe it to be.

Filling a Personal Emptiness or Need for Purpose

Similar to some of the motivations above, many Christians are trying to find identity through escapism. Missions can become the ultimate escape from a job they don't like, a dysfunctional family situation, etc. If a potential missionary struggles with belonging or is discontent with their current circumstances, it may be the case that they have a wrong motivation for being on mission.

Incorrect Exegesis of Scripture

One helpful practice is to ask potential missionaries what Scriptures have been foundational in their overseas calling. Doing so allows you to reinforce the correct application of Scripture, and it will also help you discover if they are using Scripture out of context to affirm their calling. These foundational Scriptures are likely the ones they will cite when they are sharing with the church, and they are the ones they will go back to when they need to reaffirm their calling. Therefore, it's important they interpret the Scriptures rightly at every stage of sending.

One example of a passage I have seen utilized out of context is Romans 15:20–21, in which Paul says,

> and thus I make it my ambition to preach the gospel, not where Christ has already been named, lest I build on someone else's foundation, but as it is written, 'Those who have never been told of him will see, and those who have never heard will understand

Since I live and work in Spain, this would be a convenient passage to use to affirm my calling and encourage others to come join me in the work. However, this passage is neither prescriptive as a command nor directive regarding location. It is simply a descriptive statement about Paul's desire to go to the ends of the earth, which, from his Roman-era vantage point, was Spain.

A potential missionary would be right to utilize this passage to convey their own apostolic desire to, like Paul, orient their life around taking the gospel to those who have never heard the name of Jesus. But interpreting it as a command to themselves or to others would be to read too much into what Paul is saying. Passages like Matthew 28:18–20 or Acts 1:8 are more appropriate for informing a biblical call to be sent out on mission.

Because There Wasn't Anything Else Better to Do

It is not uncommon, especially for college students or young professionals, to choose global missions as their backup option. If they don't get the job they want or have anything better to do, then global missions is their fallback plan. Anyone with this mindset needs to be challenged to consider whether God is truly calling them overseas.

Moving Healthy Potential Missionaries towards Going

While there are some who should put going overseas on hold because of improper motivations, there will be many others who should be going but have found excuses for staying. Here are some common excuses and the measures to challenge them.

I Haven't Felt Called to Go Overseas

Calling needs to be understood first through what the Bible says. Ask if they have wrestled with Matthew 28:19–20. Jesus's command to every believer is to center their lives on making disciples of all nations. Once they are convinced of its general application to their lives, you can move toward discussing the specific context in which they might be called to obey it.

I Don't Want to Raise Support

Encourage them to read *The God Ask* by Steve Shadrach. It's rare that somebody who reads this book doesn't get excited about support raising. Support raising is a great opportunity to grow in faith and build a team of prayer and financial partners. They may also consider working with organizations that fully fund their missionaries, like the International Mission Board or Samaritan's Purse. This is a good option for missionaries who either have few sources from which to raise support or whose parents are adamantly opposed to them raising support.

Going Overseas Doesn't Seem Life-Giving to Me

There can be some validity to this sentiment. If they are not passionate about reaching internationals and would really struggle to live out some key characteristics of cross-cultural workers, then it might not be for them. But take the opportunity to challenge them to consider if staying in America seems more "life-giving" just because it is familiar to them. Challenge them to cultivate a heart for missions. Teach them about God's heart for all nations.

I'm Afraid of Failing

This is a great shepherding opportunity. Isn't the fear of failure, or even actual failure itself, one of the best ways for the gospel to be demonstrated? Help them to understand that it is their obedience, not their success, that is most important. Help them to trust God to do the work through them despite their shortcomings (2 Corinthians 4:7).

I Want to Stay Close to Family

It is true that going overseas will mean being physically distant from loved ones. As missions leaders, we need to discern whether or not our potential missionaries can deal with this reality. We need to avoid guilt-tripping them. Instead, we can aim to give them a vision for how letting go of this desire could be glorifying to God.

For practical resources that go beyond what I've described in this chapter, see the Appendix for "Proactively Identifying Missionaries" and "Walking through Calling with a Potential Missionary."

The Missions Leader's Privilege

While Joe had a passion for missions, his life circumstances did not yet allow him to live out that passion in an overseas context. The missions leader at Joe and Wendy's church took the opportunity to help Joe lead his family with grace and patience. Over time, Wendy also developed a heart for the nations and also sensed God's calling to the field. While their move took place later than what Joe and the missions leader had hoped, Joe and Wendy ended up spending many healthy years on the mission field.

Missions leaders, be proactive in identifying potential missionaries and helping them discern calling. The stakes in sending missionaries are high, but the rewards for faithful sending are so much greater. God has placed you in the lives of your people to help them discern how they will make disciples of all nations.

What a privilege!

SENDING CHURCH ELEMENT #8: ASSESSING MISSIONARIES

By Nathan Sloan

> "
> *A sending church assesses potential missionaries by taking the lead (often with the assistance of a missions organization) to evaluate candidates' strengths and weaknesses and to chart a path forward toward growth. In the security of covenant membership and authentic relationship, the church partners with candidates to holistically assess their knowledge, character, and skills. Candidates are then called to intentionally enter the next phase of the sending pipeline.*

I sat the phone down, more puzzled than I had been in years. The call I had just finished was with one of our church's small group leaders. He had called to tell me that a young man in his group was moving to Tunisia that weekend to be a missionary. Exciting news, right? Not exactly.

You see, I was the missions pastor of our growing church, and I had never met this budding missionary, much less been a part of assessing and developing him for ministry. The young man in question had developed a passion for Arabic culture and knew that Tunisia needed the gospel, so he bought a plane ticket to leave as soon as he could—that weekend! He had no training, no exposure to Islam, no Arabic-speaking friends, and had never even met with a pastor at our church.

Fast forward a few days: the young man and I sat in my office and talked about his calling and his passion for missions. As I dug in, it became clear that he was not only ill-prepared for ministry in the Muslim world, but he was ill-prepared for life in general. Between relational dysfunction, spiritual immaturity, and a list of other major concerns, he had quite the journey in front of him before our church would be willing to send him overseas as a cross-cultural missionary.

I'll admit, this young man's story is extreme. Most people don't buy a one-way ticket to the Muslim world with no preparation or input from others. But this young man's story also illustrates an important principle: aspiring missionaries need assessment and development before they go overseas, and the best place for assessment and development is the local church.

Assessment and Development Are Woven Together

Over the years, I've studied missionary assessment and development and created systems for both in churches. I've come to the conclusion that these two elements are woven together. When it comes to sending missionaries from our local churches, we are always observing, assessing, mentoring, and developing those within our community for more and deeper ministry—or at least we should be.

Because assessment and development in the local church setting are often woven together, it can be hard to discuss them as separate ideas. To unpack pre-field missionary assessment and development for this book, I will write about assessment in this chapter and development in the next chapter. However, keep in mind that I will often combine the ideas because they are so interconnected.

What Is Church-Based Missionary Assessment, and Why Is It important?

A critical part of sending healthy missionaries and engaging in effective missions is assessing missionaries' knowledge, character, and skills. Holistic assessment is a vital aspect of sending and one that should be led by local churches and their leaders.

Assessment is the process of determining the quality, value, and readiness of something. In our case, it's the health and readiness of a person desiring to serve in cross-cultural missions. Church-based missionary assessment is a formal and relational process that church leaders put in place to help evaluate the health and readiness of a person for life and ministry overseas. It is evaluation, pastoral encouragement, and direction on how to grow and mature in areas that are deemed weaknesses.

What Are the Elements of a Church-Based Assessment?

Church-based missionary assessment can take on a variety of forms and structures. However, every assessment process I have seen done well within a local church included both formal and informal aspects. This two-fold dynamic of assessment provides a helpful and manageable model for local churches to assess their people for overall health and point them toward greater growth.

Informal Assessment: Relationship

Every assessment process should include informal aspects. By informal I do not mean unstructured or disorganized. The informal aspect of assessment is relational. Every effective assessment process is based on relationships with others. More than structure, classes, or a checklist, people desire to be known and seen by others. People want investment and for others to speak into their lives.

Church leaders need to take time to slow down, get to know aspiring missionaries in their midst, and observe their faithfulness as well as areas of growth. This one-on-one type of mentorship allows for a deeper investment, relational trust to be built, and more holistic assessment to happen, and it will often help the pre-field missionary be open to correction and redirection when needed.

Formal Assessment: Structured Process

Along with informal assessment, churches need well-thought-through systems of assessing pre-field missionaries. I have found that the best way to provide formal assessment and development within a church setting is through developing a sending pipeline, also sometimes called a sending process.

As we have mentioned, a sending pipeline is the formal structure a pre-field missionary needs to go through to be sent out as a missionary from that church. This structure, created by church leaders, contains all the elements of assessment and development. In the next chapter, "Developing Missionaries," I will further discuss developing a sending pipeline. For now, know that a pipeline should clearly show aspiring missionaries what it means to be sent from their local church. Assessment aspects of a pipeline may include written applications, face-to-face assessment interviews, a mentor or coach to help walk pre-field missionaries through the process, and more.

What Should We Be Looking for When We Assess a Pre-Field Missionary?

Before a local church can assess and develop a potential missionary for cross-cultural service, they need to know what they are developing toward and on what criteria they should base their assessment. Rooted in the development model of "Head, Heart, Hands" (more on this idea in the next chapter), churches should create understandable and measurable developmental markers to help bring clarity to aspiring missionaries and the church leaders who assess them. These markers—what I call a "missionary profile"—provide a picture of what could and should be when it comes to sending a healthy missionary.

Having a profile of an effective missionary is not a new concept. For generations, mission organizations and field practitioners have created lists, or profiles, of characteristics that they believed missionaries going to the field should possess. Missions leaders like Adonirm Judson,[1] Hudson Taylor,[2] and others looked for specific traits in missionaries they desired to work alongside.

During my time as a missions pastor who was assessing, developing, and sending missionaries, I created a profile of what our church was looking for in an effective missionary.[3] This profile provided our church a picture of the type of missionary we desired to send.

This is not to say that everyone we sent perfectly embodied every element of the profile. In reality, there is no such thing as an ideal or perfect missionary. God has made his people unique, and he has proven to use our uniqueness, and even weakness, for his glory. We know from Scripture that God often uses the weak and broken for his purposes. Whether it be Moses with his hesitancy to obey and fear of speaking (Exodus 3–4), Peter with his uncontrolled tongue (Mark 9:2–6) and unbelief (John 18:15–8, 25–27), or Paul and his thorn in the flesh (2 Corinthians 12:7–8), God is pleased to used his feeble people, simple jars of clay (2 Corinthians 4:7), to display his glory.

Weakness in a missionary that leads to humility and dependence on Christ is also a needed characteristic, but it should never be used as an excuse to remain in sin or immaturity. Those who have been used by God were those who grew in sanctification, maturity, and skills as they followed God and served him.

The following church-based profile of an effective missionary gives church leaders a grid, or measuring tool, to help them know what to develop people toward and on what standard we are basing our assessment of people. Assessment is based on the idea that past behavior is the best predictor of future success. As pre-field missionaries either show themselves to be satisfactory in a particular characteristic or evidence growth in maturity in that area, holistic development begins to take place, and the result is the whole person being prepared for life and ministry on the field. Each of these twelve characteristics is simply a descriptor of a broader concept that relates to cross-cultural life and ministry:

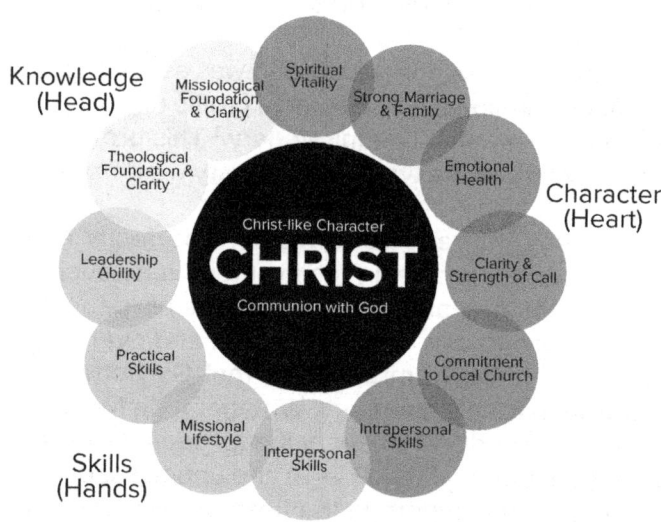

Spiritual Vitality

Spiritual vitality describes the need to have an established, healthy, and growing relationship with God. The outworking of this growing life with God can be seen in established rhythms of spiritual disciplines such as Bible reading, regular prayer, community with other Christians, rootedness in a local church, silence and solitude, Sabbath practice, and fasting, among others. However, as vital as these spiritual disciples are, a person's walk with God must not be defined solely by the outward activities they perform. Spiritual vitality is primarily rooted in a person's identity in Christ and an ongoing love relationship with him, and is seen in the sanctification of one's ordinary life.

Spiritual vitality can also be measured by means such as the fruit of the Spirit found in Galatians 5:22–24, the way a person treats others, how a person handles suffering and conflict, the victory a person has over sin, etc. As depicted in the graphic above, a person's spiritual vitality is connected to and flows from one's communion with God and ongoing development in Christ-like character.

Ryan Shaw writes, "Perhaps no other factor contributes more to the ability to produce spiritual fruit than God's powerful presence in a life. A human life filled with the presence and power of God is one of God's choicest gifts to his church and the world."[4] Not only is a life marked with the presence of God vital for ministry, but it is also vital to the health and joy of the missionary. If a person does not abide in Christ and strive to have a healthy spiritual life, everything else will eventually crumble.

Strong Marriage and Family

The characteristic of having a strong marriage and family high-lights the need to prioritize and maintain essential relationships, specifically those with one's spouse and children.[5] In 1 Corinthians 7:25–35 Paul addresses the idea that being married brings additional responsibilities to life. These are joyful responsibilities, but they must be considered when preparing for cross-cultural ministry. Church leaders need to observe and ask hard questions about the marriages and families of those they seek to send out. These questions might include: How are the pre-field missionaries loving and relating to their spouse and children? Do they have a healthy and functioning marriage? Do they give the attention and energies needed to parent well? Are they maintaining a healthy work/family balance in their everyday life?

These types of questions are important to explore with a missionary candidate before they leave for the field. Cross-cultural living can put pressures on marriage and family that, if not dealt with properly, can be devastating for a family and for a ministry team.

Emotional Health

Understanding and evaluating a pre-field missionary's emotional and mental health can be a difficult task. Local church leaders need to draw close to their pre-field missionaries, ask hard questions, and provide quality pastoral care. It would be easy to pass over this area, but emotional and mental health issues must be addressed before a person is sent. Otherwise, they are likely to arise on the field with devastating consequences. This is an area where local church leaders should put essential questions and evaluations in place.

If church leaders feel unable to address certain situations, they should refer people to mental health professionals and capable counselors. Often the best thing we can do as pastors and church leaders regarding complex mental and emotional struggles is to refer pre-field missionaries to others who are trained in these specific fields. Unpacking these issues before they leave will help the missionary have healthy responses to stress when they encounter it on the field.

Another thing for churches to consider in this area of assessment is to create a list of area counselors and mental health professionals the church recommends. Some churches have every potential missionary go through some level of pre-field counseling to improve their emotional health, check in on their marriage, or to address an issue in the past. Another benefit of having a vetted list of counselors is that you and your missionaries can reference this list when situations arise on the field or when missionaries simply need a season of counseling.

Many of the churches I've consulted with over the years use one of the many personality profiles as a means to help people grow in self-awareness and work on issues that may arise. A few of the personality profiles to consider are Myer-Briggs, DISC, the Predictive Index, and Strengthfinders. Some missions organizations will utilize psychological testing to gain a full picture of how past hurts, patterns, or trauma might affect overseas life and ministry.

Just because a person has a mental health struggle does not mean they should be disqualified from ministry overseas. It is important, however, to assess the issue, make sure they take steps to receive the appropriate help, and journey with them along the way.

Clarity and Strength of Call

Understanding a person's call to cross-cultural ministry and being confident in that call is important for health and longevity on the field. Tom Steffen defines a call to ministry as "an intense conviction that the sovereign God, through the Word, the Holy Spirit and the community of faith, has set apart a follower of Christ for participation in a specific ministry."[6]

This definition provides a healthy foundation for understanding a missionary call. However, people within the world of missions have varying ways of understanding the missionary call. Some think a special call is needed, while others believe the only prerequisites are a love for God, a commitment to the Great Commission, and a willingness to go.

Robert Speer, the well-respected late nineteenth-century missiologist, writes, "The question for us to answer is not, Am I called to the foreign field? But, Can I show sufficient cause for not going?"[7] Speer, along with many others of his day, was committed to the idea that a pre-field missionary candidate did not need a special foreign missionary call. Speer goes on to write, "The essential element of a missionary call is an openness of mind to the last command of Christ and the need of the world; and then one needs only to subject himself to the judgment of the proper authorities as to whether he is qualified to go."[8]

Local churches will have differing views of the missionary call, but what is essential here for a church-based development process is the conviction that a pre-field missionary's call should not come in isolation. A personal desire for missionary service is not the same as a call to go. A true calling must be affirmed and tested by those who have authority in sending, primarily the local church.

The local church needs to ask questions related to the call and test that call in its own context as far as it is able. Part of a healthy evaluation of call comes through examining a track record of faithfulness in the candidate's life and through evaluating their history of being resolute during trials and suffering. One helpful question to ask is, Has this person been faithful to the call on their life thus far?

Local Church Commitment

A pre-field missionary's commitment to the life of the local church is vital for a number of reasons. First, for someone to be sent, they need a home, and that takes commitment and time invested in a local church context. For a church to really send well, its members need to know the person they send and feel a certain level of responsibility that only comes through mutual commitment. My co-author Bradley Bell writes on this issue in his book, *The Sending Church Defined*: "Missionary wannabes tend to approach church leaders with a personal calling and a plan already in place—'just sign my church affirmation form and I'll be on my way,' they say. Yet covenant [with the church] calls them to not only ask what Christ's church can do for them, but what they can do for Christ's church."[9] Second, a pre-field missionary needs commitment not only to their local sending church in their home culture but also to the local church in the place to which they plan to move. This commitment to the local church on the field can take many forms. Whether it's local national church membership, membership to an international church, or joining a local house church, the outworking of love and commitment to Christ's church must be seen in how they engage the local church in their new context (if one exists there). The characteristic of local church commitment should be evident in how the prospective missionary views and values the local church of God, no matter the context, culture, ethnicity, or location.

Gerald Bates wrote an article in 1977 on the qualifications of a missionary and emphasized the need for them to be "church-oriented" people. He writes, "A missionary oriented exclusively to his profession or activity, to the exclusion of the church, risks almost certain alienation and failure."[10] Missionaries must be people in love with and committed to local churches, wherever they are.

For sending church leaders, this characteristic proves easier than some other characteristics to evaluate and develop. Church leaders can evaluate a person based on their past and present involvement and commitment to the church. Are they members? Are they active in the church and in regular community with other church members? Do they respond positively to correction and discipleship? Have they been teachable in the local church context? What do others in the church think of them?

The answers to these questions, among others, will provide clarity when asking the larger question: Is this person committed to our local church? If there is a lack of commitment, leaders should invite the pre-field missionary into greater involvement and see how they respond.

Intrapersonal Skills

Intrapersonal skills can be understood as the characteristics and skills that function within someone's mind or self. This skill set contrasts interpersonal skills that relate to the characteristics and abilities that function outwardly in relationships with others. Judith Anderson Koening defines intrapersonal skills as the "talents or abilities that reside within the individual and aid him or her in problem solving."[11] Intrapersonal skills are vital to a cross-cultural missionary because they provide the necessary tools and ability to live functionally in society, to be able to cross a culture effectively, and to function with health and success over the long term.

Koening, who is not writing with missionary development in mind, lists two broad intrapersonal skills: adaptability and self-management/self-development. Although these are helpful categories, church leaders doing missionary assessment and development need more specific categories relating to cross-cultural ministry. Some of the intrapersonal characteristics and skills necessary for cross-cultural ministry include, but are not limited to: (1) self-awareness; (2) self-control; (3) resilience; (4) adaptability; (5) flexibility; (6) perseverance; (7) teachability; (8) ability to suffer well; (9) responding well to authority; (10) spirit of humility and servanthood; (11) stress management; (12) emotional stability; and (13) displaying an inward dependence on and trust in Christ.

Interpersonal Skills

Interpersonal skills relate to the characteristics and skills needed when communicating with and relating to other people. These skills are vital in the life of missionaries because they allow them to relate to and work with their target people and with coworkers, both fellow missionaries and indigenous partners. Some of the interpersonal characteristics and skills related to cross-cultural ministry include, but are not limited to: (1) listening and learning from others; (2) displaying conflict management skills; (3) being a team player; (4) showing awareness of others' thoughts, needs, and feelings; (5) being able to relate across other cultures; (6) displaying humility and deference; (7) showing tact when dealing with others; (8) being able to forgive and move on; (9) understanding and being able to engage in social norms; and (10) displaying healthy submission to authority.

Missional Lifestyle

Developing a lifestyle of evangelism and discipleship, also known as a missional lifestyle, is an essential skill for anyone looking to serve in cross-cultural ministry. Too often, aspiring missionaries are passionate about sharing the gospel and making disciples overseas but fail to live on mission in their everyday life. In my conversations with Andy Kampman, a former missions pastor at Austin Stone Community Church, he laments the fact that the church too often sends people as cross-cultural disciple-makers when they have not proven to be disciple-makers in their own context.[12]

Local church leaders have a unique opportunity to call their members to share the gospel and make disciples in the "here and now" of their everyday lives because they live and worship with them on a regular basis. To do this well, churches can provide evangelism and discipleship training, personally model for them what these practices look like, and provide mentorship along the way to help missionary candidates grow in living missionally.

Practical Skills

For a pre-field missionary to transition to a different culture and context, and to thrive in that new setting, they need a certain set of practical skills that will vary depending on the specific culture and context in which they are working. Some skills are vital no matter where a pre-field missionary moves, such as language-learning acumen (unless they already speak the language), the ability to navigate complex cross-cultural settings, some understanding of and ability in technology, the ability to manage a budget, and more. Other skills will be determined by context, such as handyman skills, medical/first-aid training, proven business experience, or an ability to prepare meals from scratch.

These skills and many others need to be developed before a pre-field missionary leaves for the field. Not all needed skills are able to be refined in a pre-field setting, but those that are should be pursued. For church missions leaders to best understand the practical skills needed for their pre-field workers, they will need to work with missions organizations, missionaries on the field, and their missionary candidates to create a list of these skills. Once the list is determined based on the field of service, church leaders can both assess the pre-field missionary in these skills and provide pathways to learn and develop them.

Leadership Ability

Not every missionary needs to be a gifted leader, but he or she does need to possess some leadership ability. At minimum, he or she should have the ability to lead themselves and those in their family. Everyone is called upon to lead in some form or fashion at some point in their ministry; the question is, to what degree does a person desire leadership or have the ability to lead?

Determining a pre-field missionary's leadership desire and ability gives church leaders insight into proper expectations, future leadership goals, and areas of growth in the candidate's life. This characteristic can be developed in the local church setting by providing opportunities for leadership experience and responsibility within the church and through ongoing mentorship by experienced church leaders.

Theological Foundation and Clarity

As I've talked with organizational leaders and church missions leaders, there is an almost universal desire to see missionaries be well-developed in their understanding of the Bible and theology. Eric Wright quotes longtime missionary Russ Irwin when he writes, "Emphasize, emphasize, emphasize Bible training. It is needed in every type of missionary work and in all situations."[13]

Some could assume that knowing and being able to apply the truths of the Bible would be a given for those in ministry, but this is not always the case. In their book on training missionaries, Evelyn and Richard Hibbert address the value of knowing and applying the Bible in cross-cultural ministry: "Despite going to Bible college or seminary training, many of us who have served as missionaries felt unprepared for what we faced on the field ... As missionaries, we are meant to pass on our understanding of the Bible. We therefore need to know the Bible well."[14]

What better place to learn the Bible and grow in understanding and applying its truths than in the context of the local church? Through being an active leader in the church, pre-field missionaries should already be actively pursuing Bible learning and teaching opportunities. However, more specific training should be put in place.

Robust theological training can happen at seminaries or Bible colleges, but the church can provide this kind of training as well. Options for local churches include extended discipleship relationships that focus on the Bible and theology, as well as small group studies through the New Testament, theology books, or online classes.[15] These options are just a few of the many pathways of theological development any local church can offer its members.

Missiological Foundation and Clarity

Along with a good understanding of the Bible and theology, a pre-field missionary needs to be grounded in missiology, the study of missions and missions practice. While some of the lessons needed in missiology will be learned on the field, it would be unwise to send cross-cultural missionaries without first expecting them to have a foundation in missions theology, missions history, field strategy, culture and anthropology, world religions, missions trends, and specific field-related issues.

More than any other area, training in missiology can be intimidating for a local church. Few local churches have seasoned missions leaders to provide leadership in this area. This does not mean, however, that the church has to wholly outsource the task of missiological development. Local churches can, and should, take an active role in missions training in various creative ways. This might include intentional training through short-term teams, small group studies on relevant missions books, hosting an in-house missions course like *Perspectives*[16] or *You Are Sent*,[17] joining with area churches to create a practical missionary training course, or inviting a furloughing missionary to mentor pre-field missionaries.

For further guidance on effective assessment, the Appendix can direct you to the resources "Characteristics of Qualified Missionaries" and "Health Assessment & Church Interview Guide."

Assessing for Greater Growth

All the time and intentionality that goes into assessing a pre-field missionary leads to helping them move toward greater growth in areas of weakness and be more equipped to thrive in life and ministry overseas. We assess not to pass judgment but because we love our people and desire to shepherd them well. We invest, encourage, assess, and develop because we want our people to flourish in cross-cultural ministry.

Pre-field missionary assessment is not intended to be a pass-or-fail exam. We need to create assessment environments where people know we are for them, we long for them to be sent out from our churches, and we will walk with them through the process of growth.

As we assess our missionary candidates, there may be times when we need to redirect people, slow down their process, or even say no because going would be a detriment to them and to the health of the team receiving them. As hard as these conversations are, one of the greatest gifts we can give people is a clear "no" if they are not ready to go. While we may not be able to encourage them toward ministry in another part of the world, we can walk with them down a path toward deeper discipleship and spiritual health.

Every local church has a role in assessing the health and readiness of the people God calls out from among them. As you think about what this looks like in your church, spend time learning from others, reading good resources, and then developing assessment tools that fit your local church's context and needs.

SENDING CHURCH ELEMENT #9: DEVELOPING MISSIONARIES

By Nathan Sloan

> *A sending church develops missionaries when it uses the results of the assessment to help candidates grow in their readiness to be sent cross-culturally as effective disciple-makers and multipliers of the church's vision. This process includes producing a customized development plan for each candidate in the categories of knowledge, character, and skills. It also involves ongoing coaching and evaluation as missionaries move toward the field.*

"We just don't have the time, expertise, or staff to do this well."

Sadly, I've heard a version of this statement more times than I can count. I often sit with pastors and lay missions leaders, encouraging them to create a missionary sending pipeline in their church and to begin developing missionaries from within. I teach church leaders this because I fully believe that a church of any size can disciple, develop, and deploy homegrown cross-cultural missionaries. But at some point in the conversation, I often hear it: "We just don't have what it takes to pull it off."

I'll admit, though I can get frustrated with this line of thinking, I also get it. Churches are busy places, staffing and leadership are often in short supply, and global missions expertise is not easy to come by. All this can lead to the belief that theological training and missiological development are best done elsewhere, in places like seminaries and missions organizations. While there are legitimate reasons to outsource elements of theological and missiological training, there is also a vital role for the local church to fill in this process. I'll repeat my conviction: I fully believe that every church has a significant role to play in discipling, developing, and deploying cross-cultural missionaries from their body.

In fact, this is what *The Sending Church Applied* is all about: empowering the local church to take a vital role in global sending. The topics we're working through now—assessing and developing missionaries—are meant to bring greater clarity to the church's role in discipling their people toward God's global mission.

In the last chapter, I talked about the reality that assessing and developing missionaries are not two separate ideas but concepts that should be understood together. When it comes to sending missionaries from our local churches, we are always observing, assessing, mentoring, and developing those within our body for deeper discipleship and more effective ministry engagement. Knowing this, there are times I will mix the processes of assessment and development because they are so interconnected.

What Is Church-Based Missionary Development, and Why Is It Important?

It was a Tuesday morning, and I was sitting across from my professor while he searched for the words to rightly critique my writing. This was not a process I was enjoying. He was evaluating a chapter I had written on raising up missionaries in the context of the local church and found my argument lacking. Finally, he hit on something that reshaped my understanding. "Nathan," he said, "you keep talking about *training* missionaries in the local church. But when I think of training, I think of classrooms, lectures, and syllabi. Training is fine and good, but seminaries train. Missions organizations train. Local churches don't merely train people—they *develop* them. They invest in them over a long period of time. There is a difference between training and development." We went on to have a wonderful and formative conversation about the role of the church in developing missionaries. To be sure, there is a difference between training and development.

So, what is development?

Development is the process of growth and maturity in a specific area. In our case, development is the long process of discipleship, the ongoing maturity of a person's knowledge, character, and skills that lead toward health and effectiveness in cross-cultural ministry.

In the previous chapter, I unpacked a paradigm of what an effective missionary should look like. This model of an effective missionary is not primarily based on the fruit of a person's life, though fruit is important, but on the holistic picture this model provides. Remember, holistic health and readiness involves knowledge, character, and skills. These are helpful categories to use both when assessing missionaries and when helping pre-field missionaries develop toward ongoing growth and maturity.

Take a moment now to go back to the previous chapter and review the "traits of an effective missionary." Use this paradigm to help you think through the assessment and development processes for your local church. Ask yourself, What model or metric do we use to *assess* and *develop* people for life and ministry overseas? The answer to this question will determine how best to *prepare* people for cross-cultural ministry.

But before we move on to some practical ideas on missionary

development, let's consider four reasons why church-based missionary assessment is important for healthy mission practice and for the overall health of the missionary.[1]

First, the church is the primary sender of missionaries.

The task of taking the gospel to the nations was given to the church and should flow out of local churches.[2] This conviction is not a knock on the value of and need for missions organizations. They often play a significant role in missionary sending and effective field engagement. Their role, however, should be to support and empower local churches, both those that send and those that receive, in their roles of evangelism, disciple-making, and church planting.

George Peters, a noted missiologist, emphasizes this same point when he writes, "The church and not the missionary sending agency, as such, is God's authority and creation for sending forth missionaries . . . The mission agency ought to be the church's provision, instrument, and arm to efficiently expedite her task. It can neither displace nor replace the church."[3]

Second, the local church knows the pre-field missionary better than any organization, theological institution, or non-profit could.

A person's true self is revealed in the routine of daily life within the context of the local church. Through the ups and downs of ordinary life within the church, a person's character, gifts, and commitment to ministry will be discovered and cultivated. Neal Pirolo writes that the local church is the "ideal testing ground for potential missionaries."[4] Former medical missionary Thomas Hale takes this a step further when he asks, "What do the people who know you best say about you? Because the single most important factor in predicting one's future missionary performance is one's past performance as a Christian."[5]

This seems like a simple idea. Church leaders can know how a person will behave and perform in future situations based on how they have behaved and performed in the past. However, this concept is troubling to many, especially those with a romanticized view of missionary service. Often those with this view believe the myth that sharing their faith, discipling others, and life in general will become easier once they arrive on the field. Church-based development can debunk this myth by holding people accountable to a missional lifestyle here and now, in their own context, and by calling people to continual growth in all of life. The local church can and should use their intimate knowledge of pre-field missionaries to hold them to a high standard and invest in their lives, even when what needs to be said or the path toward growth is difficult.

Third, the local church is the best place to help pre-field missionaries grow.

The local church has the unique opportunity to help those within its congregation who desire to serve overseas because they live and worship with them on a regular basis. Training from missions organizations, seminaries, and parachurch organizations is great tools to utilize in developing people, but it can never replace the transformative work that the church, through the power of the Holy Spirit, can have in people's lives.

In Ephesians 4:11–16, Paul is writing to the church at Ephesus, urging them to use their gifts to build up one another toward maturity. He exhorts them "to equip the saints for the work of ministry, for building up the body of Christ, until we all attain to the unity of the faith and of the knowledge of the Son of God, to mature manhood, to the measure of the stature of the fullness of Christ" (4:12–13). Paul reminds the elders that one of their primary roles is to equip believers for ministry—to develop people who will be faithful to the work God has called them to. An outworking of this truth is seen in preparing church members for ministry overseas.

In the context of the church, potential missionaries can continue their growth and development toward possessing the traits of a healthy and effective missionary.

Finally, calling and affirmation come in community, primarily the community of the local church.

In Acts 13:1–4, a passage cited often in missions conversations, the pastors at Antioch hear from God, respond in obedience, and send out two of their own to be cross-cultural missionaries. It is important to note that Paul and Barnabas's call came in community—specifically, the community of church leaders. The New Testament model of calling and sending happens within the community of faith, the local church. Churches must not rely on missions organizations to evaluate calling and capability. Many organizations will do this well, but that does not mean churches should abdicate their responsibility to assess and develop. Local churches are the ones who know their people best and need to take a leading role in the evaluation of calling.[6]

In the book *Introducing World Missions*, Scott Moreau unpacks this idea:

> Although the one who ultimately calls or sends is God, often in the immediate context it is a local body of believers who sense or confirm a call... The body of Christ then has a significant role to play in the calling of people into ministry. As did the church at Antioch, they confirm and enact on behalf of God what the calling entails. The local body of believers, who usually best know the individual or team, should be able to affirm the call or leading and play a key role in helping the call to be fulfilled.[7]

What Should Church-Based Missionary Development Look Like?

Having laid the groundwork for church-based missionary development and established why it's so important, let's move on to what development can look like in the local church. Here are a few key ideas related to church-based missionary development.

First, know that you and your church have a lot to offer.

When it comes to preparing missionaries in our local churches, we can get fixated on what we can't offer and miss out on what we *can* offer. Every local church has significant value to offer those they send out; the trick is knowing what those things are.

For starters, if we are going to send people out to plant a church or be healthy members in churches overseas, they need to know what a healthy church is and how it functions. Church leaders should invite pre-field missionaries into the life of the church. Let them learn and develop through getting their hands dirty. Have them serve with kids, take them on hospital visits to pray with the sick, let them shadow in counseling sessions, help them learn solid Bible interpretation, and give them opportunities to teach. The opportunities for growth and development are plentiful within any local church. It just takes time to slow down and invite a pre-field missionary into the everyday, life-on-life messiness of church ministry.

Take time to think about who your church is, how God has uniquely gifted your church, and how you could invite pre-field missionaries into the beauty and grind of church ministry.

Second, know that you don't have to do it all.

On the other end of feeling like a church has little to offer is the feeling that a church has to do everything themselves. This line of thinking just isn't helpful. In reality, there are so many resources, books, and missions organizations that have expertise and are working hard to serve local churches and pre-field missionaries. Whether it's in the areas of theological education, missiology, practical experiences, or care and counseling, there are leaders and organizations out there willing to help.[8]

Finally, building out a process for sending missionaries is an important first step.

Do you remember the old baseball movie *Field of Dreams*? In it a baseball-loving farmer hears a voice one evening while walking in his cornfield. The voice urges him to build a baseball field so that Shoeless Joe Jackson and players from the past can return and play baseball once again. The voice speaks the iconic line, "If you build it, they will come."

I often think of this quote when I talk to church leaders about sending missionaries. Sometimes leaders do not know where to start or doubt whether they really could be a sending church. In this moment, I quote *Field of Dreams*: "If you build it, they will come." If you build out a sending pipeline in your church, pre-field missionaries will come.

As our Upstream leaders have served churches over the years, we have seen that the church who builds out systems of preparation often is the one that sends missionaries. When they do the work of building a pipeline of sending, pre-field missionaries in their church inevitably start popping up. That's why we advocate that every church who wants to send—no matter their size or limitations—should develop a sending pipeline.

Sending Pipeline

While sending pipelines can take on lots of forms and structures, it's important to put the pipeline in writing, make the sending process clear, and communicate it in a way so that everyone in the church understands it and what their first steps should be.

A pipeline can be simple or complex, but make sure it reflects who your church is and what your church expects in the areas of assessment and development. It is also important to make sure the pipeline you create is manageable for the leaders you have. For example, if your church's global missions ministry is led by lay leaders with limited time, it's a good idea to keep your pipeline simple and lean on the existing discipleship structure of your church to invest in your missionaries.

Over the years, Upstream has helped churches develop sending pipelines of all shapes, sizes, and complexities. We've found that almost all of these pipelines follow a similar pattern. They all have a front door (a way to start the process), measurable steps to walk through that process, and elements of assessment and development along the way. Most of these pipelines also contain different phases of development leading toward greater health and readiness for the field.

Below is the sending pipeline framework we introduced in Chapter 5, "Involving the Entire Church." This model provides key principles that churches can understand, adjust, and implement in their own context.

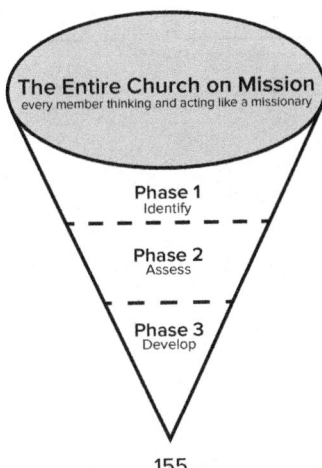

The Entire Church on Mission
every member thinking and acting like a missionary

Phase 1
Identify

Phase 2
Assess

Phase 3
Develop

As you can see, the pipeline begins with the entire church being discipled to live on mission. When this is the case, it means (in theory) that every church member has the potential to be a missionary and may at some point enter into the pipeline to explore his or her calling. The basic phases of the pipeline are then divided into the same order reflected in Chapters 7–9: identify, assess, and develop. The culmination of the pipeline is a satisfactorily developed pre-field missionary who is then affirmed and commissioned.

Although the above graphic can be helpful, each church's pipeline must be customized to fit its unique context and giftings. To give you some examples of what this customization looks like, the next two graphics are the sending processes of a couple of churches that Upstream has worked alongside.[9]

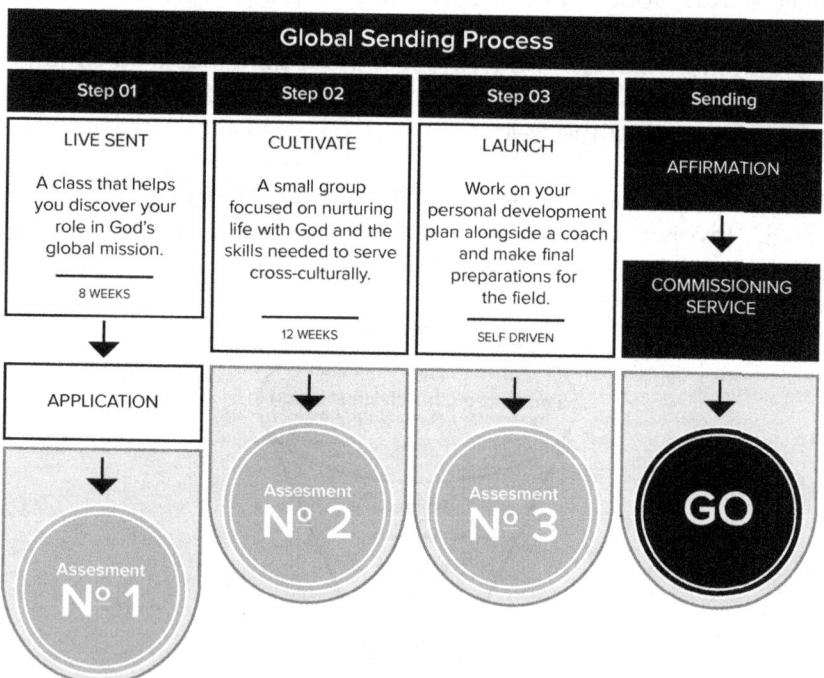

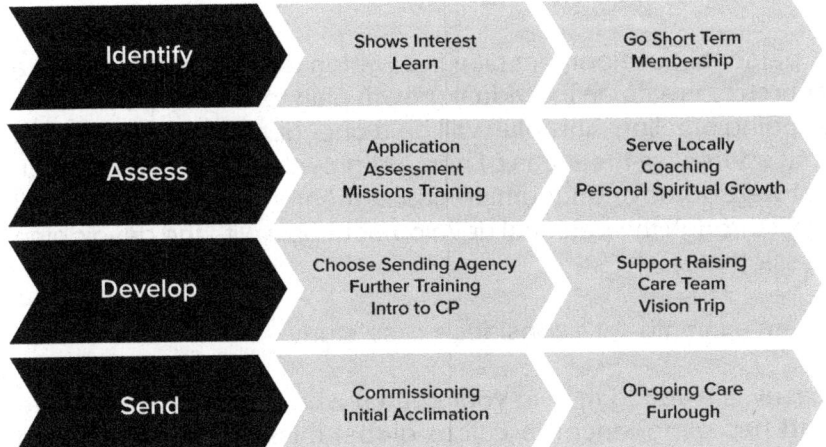

Identify	Shows Interest Learn	Go Short Term Membership
Assess	Application Assessment Missions Training	Serve Locally Coaching Personal Spiritual Growth
Develop	Choose Sending Agency Further Training Intro to CP	Support Raising Care Team Vision Trip
Send	Commissioning Initial Acclimation	On-going Care Furlough

You'll notice that both sending pipelines apply the key principles in the first framework shown above. Both pipelines have a clear starting point, distinct phases of assessment and development, and steps to walk through to be sent out.

As you think about your church, how can you adapt these principles and develop a sending process that fits your context? What can you adopt from the examples above, what do you need to adapt, and what distinctives of your church can you bring into the process?

We strongly encourage taking time to develop a sending pipeline for your local church. Make sure not to do it in isolation, but include other church leaders and friends you have in the missions world. Also, consider talking with the missions organizations you currently work with. What wisdom do they have to offer, and what can you adopt from what they already do with pre-field missionaries?

Personal Development Plans

As I mentioned before, a sending pipeline can take on all kinds of shapes and include various components. I've found two extremely helpful components to include are personal development plans and in-house mentors.

A personal development plan is a written document that allows a church to create an individual growth plan for each person in the sending pipeline. This plan will be a one- or two-page document that addresses the areas of needed growth and provides practical ways to develop them. In-house mentors are those who will walk through the personal development plan with the developing missionaries.

As an example, let's consider a case study.

Casey is a young man in your church who is faithful and mature and has experienced a call to global missions. After walking through several steps in your sending pipeline and doing a formal assessment with church leaders, the assessment team identifies that Casey has limited exposure to good missiology, is not actively sharing his faith, has a romanticized view of missions, and has unaddressed wounds in his past. You and other leaders are legitimately concerned about his potential as a cross-cultural worker, but all of these issues can be addressed through a customized development plan.

Example of a Personal Development Plan

Below is a sample personal development plan that might be written for Casey:

> Thank you for taking time to walk through the sending process of our church. Your assessment revealed the following areas that need continued growth. We have provided practical ways we want you to address these areas for development. As you review this document, please let us know if you have any questions or concerns.

+ **Missiology:** Missions and mission practice are areas of study and application that require ongoing learning. We ask that you read the following books alongside your mentor or missions pastor and regularly debrief on what you are learning: *Introducing World Missions: A Biblical, Historical, and Practical Survey* by Moreau, Corbin, and McGee and *On Being a Missionary* by Thomas Hale.

+ **Evangelism:** Enroll in our church's evangelism training and journal your gospel conversations at work and with your non-Christian friends.

+ **Theology of Suffering:** We ask that you read the following book along with your mentor or with the missions pastor and regularly debrief what you are learning: *Walking with God through Pain and Suffering* by Timothy Keller.

+ **Counseling**: Meet with one of our church's trained counselors or another Christian counselor to process the pain and hurt you experienced in college. We ask that you meet with a counselor a minimum of five times.

+ **Practical Skills:** Knowing that the team you're joining has asked that you be able to drive a manual car and be competent at cooking from scratch, we will connect you with people in the church who can teach you these skills.

This personal development plan is just an example of what you can create in your church for those preparing to go overseas (for assistance in making these plans yourself, see the Appendix's "Writing a Personal Development Plan" and "Personal Development Plan Template"). As you build out these systems, remember that missionary development takes time. This is not a class or a to-do list for people to check off. At its core, missionary development is discipleship. It's discipling people toward a greater love for Jesus and greater faithfulness to his mission.

For this reason cultivating and providing in-house mentors—especially alongside personal development plans—is absolutely essential. Remember, if you build it, missionary candidates will come, and that means you personally may not be able to walk closely alongside them all in discipleship. So look around your church for potential mentors. They don't have to have missions experience, though former missionaries often make fantastic mentors. Good mentors are mature believers who invest in others well and desire to personally participate in God's mission. It's likely that God has already provided them in your context.

Finally, as you assess and develop people within your church, remember to give grace, knowing that people often take two steps forward and one step back when preparing for life and ministry overseas. The work of development is difficult, and the church's role in this process is essential. You know your people, you love your people, and you have a vested interest in seeing them follow Jesus to the ends of the earth.

PART 3: ENGAGING PHASE

The church sends and sustains its own members.

Chapters 6 to 9 covered the Sending Church Elements in the "Developing" phase. There, you learned about the important aspects of pre-field sending: evaluating sending pathways and partners, and then identifying, assessing, and developing missionaries. This is the work of getting people into and through your sending pipeline.

Now it's time to consider the exciting reality of sending a missionary. We call Sending Church Elements #10 to #13 the "Engaging" phase because here your church is directly engaging cross-culturally with the gospel through the people you send. These chapters will guide you in commissioning your missionaries, then helping them get established, providing for their ongoing care, and maintaining your strategic focus.

10

Co
COMMISSIONING
MISSIONARIES

SENDING CHURCH ELEMENT #10: COMMISSIONING MISSIONARIES

By Bradley Bell

"

A sending church commissions missionaries by publicly setting them apart for the work to which God has called them. This communal recognition in obedience to the Holy Spirit involves worship, prayer, and the laying on of hands. It also clarifies the church's sending responsibilities and reminds the entire church of its sent identity.

If you've ever gone mountain climbing, you know the entire journey matters—packing light, starting early, sticking to the trail, staying hydrated, and finishing before dark. Nothing quite compares, however, to the moment you make the summit. It's not that the summit is the end goal; if it was, then you'd just stay there once you arrived. The summit is climactic because it divides the experience in half. Before you get there, where do your eyes often look? Up to the summit. After you leave, where do you tend to gaze in the distance? Back to the summit. It's *the* pivotal point of the entire journey.

Commissioning is like the summit of sending. Let us be clear here: *commissioning is not the end goal.* Unfortunately, many churches treat it that way, seeing commissioning as their last act of direct involvement before committing the missionary entirely to the care of a missions organization. Some churches even forgo commissioning altogether, either because the missionary will be "appointed" by their organization, or simply because they don't see it as a momentous occasion. This is tragic!

While it is not the end goal, commissioning is the pivotal point of the entire sending journey. It's the summit to which potential missionaries should look forward and the summit to which sent missionaries should look back. Most notably, it puts the church at the center of sending.

In numerous places throughout the book, we have referenced Acts 13:1–4, a passage that is significant to sending. It serves as one of the Bible's clearest examples of commissioning missionaries. There we read,

> Now there were in the church at Antioch prophets and teachers, Barnabas, Simeon who was called Niger, Lucius of Cyrene, Manaen a lifelong friend of Herod the tetrarch, and Saul. While they were worshiping the Lord and fasting, the Holy Spirit said, "Set apart for me Barnabas and Saul for the work to which I have called them." Then after fasting and praying they laid their hands on them and sent them off. So, being sent out by the Holy Spirit, they went . . .

This may seem like only a momentary prelude to the grand missionary journey on which Barnabas and Saul are about to embark. But let's take a closer look and consider how it casts a vision for an entire Sending Church Element.

Commissioning Takes Place in the Context of the Local Church

This is perhaps the clearest observation from the text. For decades it has been normal practice for missionaries to be commissioned (or "appointed") primarily by their missions organization. While it certainly makes sense for missions organizations to celebrate the appointment of missionaries, the biblical practice of commissioning is given in the context of the local church. That is where Barnabas and Saul were commissioned. It was also where they returned after finishing their work, specifically because it was "where they had been commended to the grace of God for the work that they had fulfilled" (Acts 14:26).

Notice that in 13:3 we are told "they [the church] laid their hands on them and sent them off." Then, in the very next verse, we read, "So, being sent out *by the Holy Spirit*, they went" (emphasis mine). This raises the question, were they sent out by the church or the Spirit? The only answer that's faithful to the text is ... both! It seems that the singular act of commissioning is actually the dual commitment of the church in submission to the Spirit. If the Spirit affirms that the local church is central in commissioning, then so should we.

Commissioning Occurs Because of the Communal Recognition of God's Calling

Notice that the Holy Spirit didn't just speak to Barnabas and Saul about *their* missionary call but also spoke to (at least) all the prophets and teachers at Antioch (and perhaps the entire church). Then, they seem to confirm this calling with further fasting and prayer (13:3). Thus, commissioning should be the culmination of a communal process, the public affirmation from multiple church leaders and members that the missionaries are indeed called and qualified.

In the terms we have used thus far in this book, the "communal process" is the pre-field sending pipeline of identification, assessment, and development (see Chapters 7–9). While we don't see these specific terms in the Book of Acts, they are present in concept through the story of Antioch, especially in the life of Saul. Barnabas had proactively identified Saul as a leader and teacher (Acts 11:25). No doubt the effect of his character and gifting was assessed by the congregation during that time (Acts 11:26). Saul was then developed as the church sent him and Barnabas to deliver relief to the church in Judea (Acts 11:29–30). Surely, all this led to Antioch's recognition of God's apostolic calling on Saul. Together they could say of his commissioning, similar to the words of Acts 15:28, "It has seemed good to the Holy Spirit and to us." That's the spirit you want to see as your church commissions those they send.

Commissioning Is a Sacred Event That Includes Worship and Prayer

We can only imagine how momentous it was for the church at Antioch to send out two of their very best and beloved leaders. The only way they could have made such a sacrifice would have been by maintaining their view of the supreme worth of Christ. It would also have necessitated a deep understanding of the nations' need for the gospel and the daunting nature of the task. Thus, worship and prayer remind both the sending church and those being sent that the glorious risen Christ has all authority in heaven and earth, and that we are sent in that authority (Matthew 28:18–19a). It also demonstrates their dependence upon "the Lord of the harvest" (Luke 10:2). Although few churches include this measure today, fasting was clearly included in Antioch's worship and prayer. Imagine the impact of your entire church fasting together as part of commissioning!

Another visible sign of healthy commissioning is actually *tears*. Although Luke doesn't mention tears at Antioch's commissioning, he does give us a glimpse into Paul's goodbye among the Ephesian elders: "And there was much weeping on the part of all; they embraced Paul and kissed him, being sorrowful most of all because of the word he had spoken, that they would not see his face again. And they accompanied him to the ship" (Acts 20:37–38). Sending is a bittersweet business. If the missionary candidates have put down the deep roots of loving relationships, then despite the excitement that lays ahead, there will be sorrow in the "see you later." If the sending church has invested faithfully in the missionary candidates and benefitted from the fruit of their gifts, then there will be sorrow in the farewell. The tears at a commissioning are a sacred gift to God.

Commissioning Involves Laying on of Hands

The act of laying on hands has a rich biblical history. In the Old Testament, it marked the transfer of authority and wisdom (Numbers 27:23; Deuteronomy 34:9). In the New Testament, it is associated with receiving the Spirit (Acts 8:17), healing from blindness (Acts 9:17), baptism (Acts 19:6), receiving a spiritual gift for ministry (1 Timothy 4:14), and restoring a person to the church (1 Timothy 5:22). In Acts 13 it represents the church's recognition of the Holy Spirit's calling, Barnabas and Saul's appointment as representatives of the church, and the belief that God would bless them. In light of this, it will be meaningful not only to lay hands on the missionaries but also to explain why the church is doing so.

There are different ways that churches can go about this based on their size and tradition. Some welcome the entire church to come and lay on hands together. Others invite the church to come individually to speak a word of affirmation. Some churches have only the elders lay on hands. Others invite family members and friends to join in. Whatever your approach, it's meaningful and biblical to lay on hands as part of commissioning.

Commissioning Is the Beginning of the Journey, Not the End

Because we have the benefit of knowing that Barnabas and Saul returned to Antioch when the work to which they had been commissioned was fulfilled (Acts 14:24–28), we can see how Antioch's relationship with these missionaries was ongoing. Their commissioning was not the end of the church's participation in global missions—it was more like the beginning. To borrow an analogy from Jesus, it's not fitting to lay our hands on the plow and then look back or let go (Luke 9:62).

Thus, commissioning is more than a holy goodbye. There are certainly times in the life of the church when we offer a prayer of blessing for those who are departing indefinitely. But that is not commissioning. Commissioning indicates a commitment not just to warm regards but also to an ongoing, reciprocal relationship. The missionary is being sent, not released.

Commissioning Is Recognized as a Dual Commitment

It is common for a traditional commissioning to unintentionally place the missionaries on a pedestal. The result is that church members can easily walk away impressed by the calling of the missionaries and yet dejected about their own calling as local sent ones (i.e., "I could never be like them."). Instead, commissioning should be holistic and reinforce everyone's commission to be faithful witnesses, regardless of context. This is not only achieved by including rich sending theology, but also by the missionaries' honesty regarding the joys and the struggles in being sent. This approach seems counterintuitive, but it will limit the idealism of the missionary pedestal by effectively putting everyone on the same playing field (i.e., "Wow, I am like them, because they're imperfect too.").

This approach also allows the sending church to be commissioned as "fellow workers for the truth" (3 John 1:8) in their support of the missionaries. Yes, the missionaries certainly "take the stage" at a commissioning, but the sending church should too, in a sense. Remember, the Spirit's calling of missionaries in Acts 13 actually came in the form of a command *to the church*: "Set apart for me Barnabas and Saul for the work to which I have called them" (13:2b). Thus, attention should be given to the church's specific ongoing responsibilities to help members understand their role in sending and feel its gravity. In this way, commissioning is clearly a dual commitment.

Sending Covenant

One of the most practical ways to achieve this understanding of dual commitment is with what we call a sending covenant. Some churches refer to it as a "memorandum of understanding" (MOU) or simply a sending agreement. Although these terms are helpful in the context of organizations and businesses, calling it a covenant more effectively captures the spirit of the commitment. It is more than a contract—it is a sacred agreement entered into before the Lord by both the sending church and the missionaries.

Because the sending church and the missionaries have been given the same Spirit and brought into the same body, their commitment to one another is enduring. A missions organization commits to the relationship for as long as the missionaries are appointed by them. A church, however, commits to the relationship for the long haul, come what may. Their aim isn't just effective missionaries but whole persons conformed more and more to the image of Christ until the day they meet him face to face.

A sending covenant, then, clarifies the specifics of the sending relationship. It allows both parties to understand exactly what they are responsible for. Assumptions are one of the biggest threats to the relationship between the sending church and the missionaries. The covenant not only sets expectations, but it also gives grounds for breaking the agreement (that is, breaking the covenant, not the relationship). This is extremely important if and when the relationship drifts because of either party's shortcomings.

Before giving an example of a sending covenant, it's important to note that the process of writing and agreeing upon a covenant should happen well before the commissioning itself. Church leadership should meet with the missionaries to review and discuss the covenant to ensure everyone is on the same page. After all, the missionaries deserve to have a voice in that to which they're committing.

Once the draft is agreed upon, it should be finalized in a document that both the sending church and the missionaries can sign and keep. Here is an example:

The sending church commits to:

+ Praying for the missionaries and the people they serve in Sunday services, small groups, households, and among the missionary care team.
+ Overseeing and cultivating the effectiveness of advocates to care for the missionaries.
+ Providing care visits with the goal of one per term.
+ Being available as pastors and advocates to provide care and counsel. Advocates will communicate any such requests to the pastors.
+ Maintaining sensitivity to secure communication.
+ Providing logistical support and opportunities to report during stateside visits.
+ Providing ongoing financial support as agreed upon before commissioning.

The missionaries commit to:

+ Recognizing and relating to the sending church

as having a significant, ongoing role in their life and ministry.

+ Continuing to participate in the life of the sending church through relationships, prayer, and giving of resources.

+ Responding in a timely manner to communication from the pastors and advocates.

+ Sending monthly updates for the sake of ongoing relationships and prayer.

+ Maintaining open and honest communication with the advocates.

+ Spending one-third of their stateside visit in the sending church's city in order to participate in the life of the church.

As mentioned earlier in this chapter, commissioning should be recognized as a dual commitment, and the sending covenant is useful for facilitating this. In other words, it allows for both the missionaries *and* the sending church to be commissioned. During a central part of a Sunday service, the specifics of the covenant are displayed on a screen and/or written in a bulletin for all to see. As expected, the missionaries then stand before the congregation and publicly vow with God's help to keep their part of the covenant. But then—and this a powerful moment—you ask the congregation to stand before the missionaries and publicly vow with God's help to keep *their* part of the covenant. Faithful sending commissions everyone.

If you want to leverage commissioning to benefit the entire church's sent identity, consider a "Commissioning Sunday." This is an entire Sunday service devoted to sending. This might include missional liturgy, worship songs, and a sermon focused on global missions. Some sending churches allow the missionaries to choose the worship songs and participate in serving communion (since it will be their last opportunity to worship with the church for a long time). You can even top off the gathering with a fellowship meal or reception. This is, of course, if security allows for these public measures. If the missionaries are being sent to high-risk locations, then it may be better to commission in less public settings.

As you can imagine, making this kind of effort can have a lasting impact on everyone in the church. This is more than just putting the spotlight on one ministry in the church over all the others. It's celebrating the beauty of our sending God and the joy of participating in his mission together, an emphasis that can inform every ministry in the church.

For further help with commissioning well, see the Appendix's "Commissioning Examples" and "Sending Commitment Template."

Hit the Trail

I don't know about you, but I remember well the mountaintops I've summited. On my way up a 12,000-foot pinnacle in East Africa, I struggled for oxygen and nearly decided to quit. However, the view from the top and the exhilaration of being there was totally worth a little altitude sickness ... and some sore feet. I'd do it again tomorrow!

What might happen in your church if commissioning was viewed as the summit of sending—not as the end goal but as the pivotal moment that divides the sending journey in half? Sure, it may require some thoughtful effort and result in a few tears. But just as we're still talking about Acts 13:1–4 all these years later, commissioning could be an unforgettable experience for your church and missionaries. So hit the trail, and see what God does.

SENDING CHURCH ELEMENT #11:
GETTING MISSIONARIES ESTABLISHED

By Larry McCrary

> *A sending church gets missionaries established in partnership with their missions organization by staying in close communication during the first term. Aware of the possibility of attrition, the church encourages them to remain faithful through the rigors of language and culture acquisition rather than returning home prematurely.*

In 2019 I ran my first marathon in the beautiful coastal city of Nice, France. I had trained hard for nine months, putting in the long miles necessary to prepare. I knew I would not set any land speed records, but I also knew that I would set a personal record if I finished the race. I had a race day strategy. The week of the race I watched what I ate, hydrated well, and kept myself limber as we took in the scenery.

The morning arrived for my race. As I traveled to the starting line, a storm was moving in from the ocean. When I got there, it started to pour. It did this for the next hour, damaging roads, flooding some of the race path, and delaying the start of the race. The cleanup postponed the race even further.

Finally, the starting gun sounded, and we were off. Within a minute of our start, another storm blew in, and we were in the middle of it. I had not signed up to run my first marathon in a storm on the Mediterranean. It was windy, stormy, and rainy for the first ten kilometers (6.2 miles)—terrible running conditions. All we could do was keep running and hope for the best. I had to find a way to run the entire 26.2 miles.

How I started the marathon was critical. I knew it would take more energy to run in the rain. I had to mentally adjust for a different type of race. The peace and tranquility I had expected turned into a wet and windy grind. To make it the entire distance, I had to remember what my coach taught me: stay relaxed at the start, don't let other runners affect my pace, and stay hydrated. I had to remember to start off at a relaxing pace where I could build up without getting caught up in the energy of the racers—and without trying to outrun the storm!

Similarly, no matter how much planning and preparation a sending church and a missionary do, there will be storms as they start. There are too many factors at play for this not to happen. The early days can make or break a missionary. Having a sending church that shows concern and demonstrates healthy care during these early months or years can significantly impact their fruitfulness long term.

Thankfully, we have not been left to figure out this process on our own. The New Testament gives us examples of instructions and assistance being given to those who are sent. These examples can serve local churches in helping them get their missionaries established.

Preparation for the Task at Hand

In Luke 10:1–8, when Jesus sends out the seventy-two disciples, he strategically sends them two by two to the places he was about to go. While we cannot make a prescription from a descriptive passage, I think it is significant that Jesus sent them in pairs. Likewise, in Acts 13:4–5 we see that Paul and Barnabas were sent out as a team along with John Mark. We can learn from these examples that missions is not a solo task, but one accomplished in community.

Jesus gave a few instructions for what would lie ahead for these disciples whom he sent out. vv He even warned them that they would be like lambs among wolves. This is not a pretty picture. It represents the certain dangers Jesus's disciples would face as they went out in obedience to him.

He instructed them to pack lightly and not get distracted from the task at hand. When they entered a house, he told them to bless it and give it peace. They would know if they were being received and if they should move on. He told them to expect that some would show hospitality and that they should receive the blessings and hospitality well. He wanted them to invest where they were accepted and not move around. Go deep. Eat what they put before you.

Though we have the Great Commission, we do not have the benefit of being in Jesus's physical presence like the seventy-two disciples. I often wonder what it would be like to have Jesus doing our pre-field training!

Furthermore, how cool would it be for Jesus to be the one who debriefs us when we return? As the disciples returned, in awe of all that had happened, he reminded them of their identity—that their names were written in the Book of Life. They belonged to Jesus, which he wanted them to fully understand. This passage in Luke 10 can help us be confident that our identity in Christ is most important. We belong to him.

While Luke 10 is not meant to be an exhaustive list of all that will happen on the mission field, it does provide a helpful preview of the journey. The Sender gives the seventy-two disciples some inside information on what to expect. As a sending church and a missions leader, you can also help shape and form the missionaries before, during, and after their service. Your church can help them get started on the right foot by coming alongside them in the preparation and development phase, giving them resources and a lifeline of support as they go.

Connecting with the Receiving Team

Another example we would point out from Scripture is the story of a maturing Christ-follower named Apollos in Acts 18:24–28.

Apollos, who was from Egypt, came up to Ephesus. He had a great knowledge of the Scriptures. He had been discipled, but he only knew of the baptism of John. He had a lot of passion and gave solid teaching about Christ. After Priscilla and Aquila (the tentmakers who collaborated with Paul on mission) met him in the synagogues, they invited him into their house to instruct him further. Among other things, they likely helped expand his understanding of baptism. Apollos went on from there and continued his journey of sharing and teaching about Jesus to other cities.

I want to highlight two aspects of this passage. First, the leaders in the church of Ephesus must have known that Apollos wanted to be an itinerant teacher of the gospel. Priscilla and Aquila saw the qualities of Apollos, but they also noticed a theological point that needed to be reframed, so they invested in him. He must have received the exhortation well because we see him continuing in his ministry later in these passages. The church was encouraged by his desire to take the gospel further. This is a great example of senders identifying a potential sent one and making the effort to pour into his or her life.

Secondly, it is important to note that the disciples in Ephesus wanted Apollos to go. They felt encouraged by him and affirmed him moving onward. But they also wanted to write a letter of recommendation to the disciples in Achaia asking them to welcome him. For some reason, they felt it was important to write this letter for him to carry with him so that when he arrived, the disciples would receive him well. We do not know the full impact the letter had, but we do read that Apollos had a fruitful ministry where he went.

Up to this point, we have focused on the sending church establishing the proper foundation for missions identity, vision, and strategy. We see the importance of identifying and assessing potential missionaries and developing them as cross-cultural workers. We commission them and send them on their way. As those who have invested in and know them well, just like Priscilla and Aquila to Apollos, it only makes sense that we would continue that investment through this critical stage. We shouldn't discontinue our interest and care and expect the missions organization to pick up our slack. Instead, we can and should work in tandem with the missions organization as they help our missionaries adjust to their team and new city.

Part of evaluating a missions organization and field partner well is ensuring they have a good plan for cultural adaptation, language learning, and team integration. At this point, they do not know your missionary like you do, so you should work with that team leader and missions organization to care for that missionary. Unlike the church in Ephesus, we do not have to write a letter for our missionaries to carry with them. We have the blessing of being able to connect with them over video, or even visit them in these early stages. Your care as a sending church can be vital for helping them establish this new relationship with the receiving team.

A Lot of Moving Parts

Moving cross-culturally is much different than moving within your own culture. Many unique changes and challenges hit missionaries simultaneously as they land in their city. They have to:

- » find places to eat
- » figure out how to navigate their new city
- » learn logistics in an overseas context
- » learn the local language
- » learn the culture
- » understand the context
- » adjust to family life overseas
- » develop their strategy for their ministry
- » integrate into team life

It is a daunting list. It takes time, but getting off to the right start is critical so that missionaries not only survive but begin to thrive as well.

The first few years of missionary life are often the most critical for determining their likelihood of remaining on the field long-term. Missionaries who are able to find a way to adjust to their new life and learn how to thrive amidst the challenges listed above often do well. However, the journey will rarely be without a lot of trial and error.

Early in our career overseas, I asked a missionary couple with thirty years of experience about longevity and how they made it on the field for so many years. The woman replied with a simple but profound statement. She said, "Because neither of us wanted to get on the plane on the same day."

Anyone who has lived overseas has had what we call "airplane days." These are days when we are ready to pack it up, get on the airplane, and head back home. We have reached a tipping point, and we feel the best solution is to go back. These days are difficult for missionary couples, even if it's only one spouse who is feeling this way. It's even more difficult for singles who may not have someone they feel close enough with to share their struggles.

Even if they have a healthy team, missionaries may fear how their team members will react to them sharing their struggles.

On these dark days, it is vital that missionaries have a sending church that can encourage them, challenge them, and remind them of their calling. Sure, some people need to return home, sometimes earlier than expected. However, the sending church should be such an integral part of their missionaries' lives that a decision to return is never made alone.

How Can the Sending Church Help Out in This?

It is essential for missionaries to know that they have a sending church that is behind them—one that does more than financially support them. They need their church to pray for them, communicate with them regularly, and provide accountability and ongoing care. This creates a healthy sending relationship.

Below are some practical and meaningful ways your church can minister to your missionaries in their early days to help them get started well.

Talk to them. Have a plan for how to communicate with them upon arrival. Connect with them briefly through calls, video, or text. There are many ways that we can show them support early on through technology. (Be sure to have security in mind and find out the best way to communicate with them on the field in a secure manner.)

Do not talk to them too much. While it is important to talk to them, we don't want to overwhelm them or create dependency on us. We want them to transition to relying on the day-to-day leadership of their team and lean into important aspects of learning culture and language. If we over-communicate, we risk keeping the connection so tight that they never fully embrace their new culture. There is a balance between letting them know you are there for them and giving them space to do all they need to do in their new home. Their number one job is getting settled in and starting the process of embracing their new life.

Visit them during their first term. We love seeing the sending church do a member care or vision visit during their first term. However, we would encourage you to wait until they have completed their language learning requirement and have determined the basics of their field strategy. While short-term trips are valuable, they take a lot of preparation and work on the field side, especially when missionaries are still in language learning.

Taking a vision and care trip with key leaders from the sending church and close friends of the missionary is the most valuable first-term trip. It creates the opportunity for trouble-shooting early issues, getting to know the rest of the team, and reinforcing the commitment to each other.

Write to them with real stationery. It is super easy to send gift cards, and believe me, we enjoy gift cards. However, there is nothing like getting an actual piece of mail in our mailbox. My wife has worked extensively with third culture kids (TCKs) as a teacher and educational consultant. She once did an informal survey with a class of TCKs, and at the top of the list of what made them feel cared for was receiving a physical card or a package from their home church.

What We See Some Churches Doing

A church Upstream has coached in sending over the years had a college student who wanted to study abroad in Europe. The student did not simply want to study abroad; she wanted to live on mission while she was there. The sending church worked through their connections and helped her find a missions team to partner with in the city where she would be studying for accountability, community, and strategic direction.

The missionary team was located on the other side of this very large city from her university, and transportation was expensive. The church covered the cost of that transportation because they believed the local team connection was essential to her getting established and for overall flourishing.

Another church had a marketplace missionary couple who moved to the Middle East. The company paid for the employee to learn the language, but not the spouse. The church knew it would be valuable to this couple's long-term sustainability and effectiveness for the spouse to learn the language as well, so they decided to pay for the language school so the spouse could learn the language and make better inroads to the culture.

These are two examples where missionaries were not connected with a missions organization and truly needed the church to help them get established. There are also great examples of how churches, in partnership with the missions organization, have helped missionaries get established.

For instance, one church makes it a priority to visit missionaries during their first term. Generally, they send a couple who are good friends or mentors of the missionaries simply to love them, encourage them, pray for them, watch their kids so they can go on a date night, walk around their area and dream with them, and have fun with them. It is a great way for the church to minister to their missionaries, especially during the first term when they are experiencing culture shock and large amounts of "failure" through the language- and culture-learning phase.

My wife and I wrote a book called *First 30 Daze: Practical Encouragement for Living Abroad Intentionally* in which we give thirty days of devotions and application points for missionaries landing on the field to read during their first month. These points give some practical ideas but primarily focus on helping the missionary develop the right posture towards their new life. For an additional resource that cultivates this posture, see the Appendix's "Learning Missionary Skills (IPOC3)."

Another church buys a copy of *First 30 Daze* for each of their missionaries and each member of their advocate team (more on these teams in Chapter 12). The entire team was encouraged to read the book during the missionary's first thirty days on the field. It provides a daily guide to pray with them on the topic addressed for that day, and it also gives them a picture of what their missionary is encountering on the field.

And for one more example, when we first moved to the field in 2001, our sending church helped us connect with our new overseas community by providing encouragement and funding to join local groups in the city. In many city-focused missions contexts, joining clubs for fitness, sports, art, or music is a great way to enhance your language learning and culture acquisition and to begin to build relationships. Plus, it can be refreshing for your soul and body.

On-Ramping Plan

As missionaries enter the field, one thing that can get confusing for them is the role that each entity plays in their day-to-day lives. There's the sending church, the missions organization, the team leader, and themselves. Keeping communication flowing between these entities can be a challenge. Get to know the team leader beforehand so that there is open communication and established expectations for the responsibilities of each entity. Consider writing up a memorandum of understanding (MOU) that outlines the roles each entity will fill. This isn't a legal document; it's simply an outline that will help each party remember their responsibilities.

The Appendix can direct you to an Upstream resource for churches, missionaries, and the organization to establish a "90-Day On-Ramping Checklist for Newly Launched Missionaries." This will help each entity know what needs to be done for each day as the missionaries arrive. We have found this to be a great way to facilitate communication and partnership in helping the missionaries more quickly acclimate to their new life.

Troubleshooting When Things Get Hard

When things get hard for your missionaries, what do you do? How can you help them? Here are some of the common challenges that we've seen missionaries run into in their first term and some ways you can walk through them together.

Language Learning Is Not Going Well

It is not unlikely that the missionary you have sent from your church got excellent grades in high school and college but will still fail their first language class. Some missionaries might not succeed in the classroom environment for language learning. Or maybe your missionaries are utilizing a tutor or an auditory learning method and the lack of structure is counterproductive to their learning style. Maybe they are in the right learning environment, but the stress of moving cross-culturally and learning a new language is repeatedly knocking them down. Maybe one spouse is succeeding while the other is falling further and further behind. How can you help them?

Pre-field, it's important to conduct a language-learning assessment and provide training on how to learn a language. Check with the missions organization to see what training they provide (if any). If they don't offer any or you feel it might not be sufficient, connect with organizations that specialize in language and culture training. Reach out to our team if you need some referrals. There are many around.

Ensure that the missionaries come away understanding what type of learning style they have and what type of language-learning will best suit them. Will they do best in a classroom setting, with a private tutor, or using an auditory learning method? This is important to know going into the assignment. Just because a language learning technique worked for a team leader, it does not mean that's the one your missionaries should follow.

If they are struggling on the field, consider connecting them with a language coach who can assess how they are doing and what they might practically change in their learning mode, schedule, etc. One size does not fit all. And don't let money be the issue. Spending a few thousand dollars on a coach, tutor, or language assessment is a drop in the bucket if it allows them to stay on the field long-term.

Some missions organizations may have a one-size-fits-all approach to language learning that does not provide the flexibility to utilize other methods. When evaluating missions organizations, it is important for you to find out if they have some flexibility based on learning styles. If they do not, you may want to consider whether it is the right organization to move forward with.

If you are currently in this situation with one of your missionaries on the field, it will be valuable for you to come alongside them to help the team leader or organization understand why your missionaries would benefit from a different language-learning method. Ultimately, you'll need to submit to the organization's protocol, but they might be open to supplementing the missionaries' language learning with another method if (1) there is one available, (2) your church is willing to assist with funding for it, and (3) it would not impede their other work.

Relational Struggles with the Team Leader or Team Members

This is one of the most common issues I've observed on the field. The team leader has to balance the roles of boss, friend, family, and confidant. It's a difficult tightrope to walk. Inevitably, there will be some tension with a team leader. It can be difficult for team members to suddenly gain a new friend and co-worker with little to no prior relational connection. Add in the cross-cultural stress, and Satan can wreak havoc. How can you help your missionaries navigate these struggles?

Pre-field, we know assessing and developing our missionaries to deal with relational conflict is important. Refer to Chapters 8 and 9 for more on how to do this. As we learned from Chapter 6, we also want to choose great missions organizations and team leaders. We do not select them simply for what they do, but for what they value. If your church and the team leader have similar values for ministry, then you have common ground to work from.

As much as possible, get to know the team leaders and team members. This will better help you mitigate relational challenges and give you some relational trust moving into a conflict.

After they arrive on the field, the missionary may have struggles with their team leader. Don't take their side too quickly. As one who has dealt with numerous on-field conflicts, Proverbs 18:17 has been a great source of wisdom: "The one who states his case first seems right, until another comes and examines him." There truly are two sides to every story.

Encourage your missionaries to find ways to respectfully submit to their leaders. As Hebrews 13:17 says, "Obey your leaders and submit to them, for they are keeping watch over your souls, as those who will have to give an account. Let them do this with joy and not with groaning, for that would be of no advantage to you."

Work to ask good questions of your missionaries so they have another trusted voice in their life. Some of the questions include:

> » What is going on in your life right now that might be causing you to react in this way?
> » What can you take from your team leader's statement, even if it was communicated poorly?
> » Is there anything you need to apologize for?
> » Is there anything you need to say to them to help them understand your point of view?
> » Is this only a tension to endure or a problem that

must be solved?

When necessary, you may need to guide your missionaries to find a new team if the team leader demonstrates a lack of good character. However, this should be a last resort.

The Vision Is Different Than What Was Expected

It's challenging for team leaders to communicate vision and nearly impossible for them to have an answer for every known and unknown expectation missionaries might have pre-field. Undoubtedly, your missionaries will face unmet expectations. How can you help them navigate this when it happens?

Pre-field, ask the team leader for a vision/strategy statement and/or a job description for your missionaries. These are helpful reference points for differentiating what was communicated and what was assumed. Additionally, help your missionaries identify their expectations as best they can. Write all of them down together. Identify what is *core* to the mission and what is *peripheral*. Help them hold tightly to what is the *core* and loosely to what is *peripheral*. While the peripheral can affect the missionaries' experience, the important thing is whether or not it affects their ability to do what they are called to do.

Unmet expectations generally come to light after a few months on the field. They are compounded by the stress of moving overseas. These unmet expectations often lead to doubt about one's calling and blame-shifting toward their leadership. As a missions leader, with pre-field documents in hand, you can ask questions that help the missionaries identify where the expectation is not being met. You can help them identify if it is a core or peripheral expectation. If it is a core issue, then it needs to be addressed with the team leader. You can encourage them to have that conversation with their supervisor and, if need be, assist them in it.

If it is a peripheral issue, then we need to ask good questions of our missionaries, such as:

» Is this issue impacting your ability to thrive? If so, how? If not, then how can you work through it?
» If this expectation continues to go unmet, how will you handle it?
» What else in your life is causing you stress at this moment? Is that stress leading you to add an unnecessary expectation on others?
» Are you asking God to shape your expectations?
» Are you unnecessarily shifting any blame for how you're feeling onto your supervisor?

As missions leaders, we can care for our people by encouraging them to look inward and take responsibility for their own response to an experience.

Little Responsiveness amongst the People

A lack of responsiveness can certainly be hard, but almost every missionary runs into this issue at some point. The good news is that it is something they can walk through with others. How can you help them navigate this challenge?

Pre-field, make sure they understand the spiritual soil in their country of service. Make sure they have shown faithfulness to God's mission before they leave for the field. Remind them that it is ultimately God's work to save souls, but that he uses people to accomplish his mission (2 Corinthians 3:5–6).

After arriving on the field, you can bring them back to these truths. You can encourage prayer and faithful evangelism. Lack of fruit is not an uncommon reason for missionaries to leave the field, so it will be important for you to keep up with those who are serving in areas where responsiveness to the gospel might be low.

The Environment Is Harder Than Expected

Overseas ministry can be really hard. Whether it's the heat, the cold, the smells, the lack of personal space, the absence of familiar cooking ingredients, the transportation difficulties, or the attitudes of the people, the difficulties of ministering in another culture can wear on missionaries. Likely, it will not just be one of these things but a multitude of different factors accumulating that will put them over the edge. How can you help them not get overwhelmed by the difficulties of life and ministry in a foreign context?

Pre-field, make sure the missionaries are raising enough support to provide flexibility. Doing so will allow them to make adjustments with schooling for their kids, housing, transportation, and more. When there isn't enough funding to be flexible, missionaries can begin to feel trapped.

After they arrive, help your missionaries think about ways they might be making things too hard on themselves. Reminding your missionaries of their limitations and expectations is important. Help them think through ways they might make their lives easier while still being good stewards of their time and money. They need to remember that everything overseas takes about four times as long to do as it would in their home country, if not more.

While taking a bus might save some money, a taxi saves time. Time is a precious commodity overseas. If the housework is bogging down one of the spouses, consider having them hire a house helper. While this might feel like a luxury, it offers many potential benefits for their time, ministry, and sanity. It is better to stay on the field with a house helper than to leave the mission field because of a personal philosophy about what missionaries are and aren't allowed to spend money on.

The Missionary Seems Out of Their Mind

Because cross-cultural adjustment and living is so stressful, we have seen some missionaries begin to separate themselves from reality. The challenges of adjusting to life overseas can lead to some uncharacteristic thinking and actions. The stress can cause them to develop alarming patterns of bitterness, anger, anxiety, blame-shifting, moral failure, and distortion of reality. How can you help them through this time?

It is hard to predict how your missionaries will deal with life on the field. I've seen those I felt a little uneasy about sending totally thrive and those I thought would do amazing totally collapse. This is why pre-field missionary assessment and development is so important. Talk thoroughly with the missions organization about your potential missionaries while they are still in the beginning stages of sending. Lean on the organization's guidance and expertise. Consider the benefits of psychological testing and counseling, not just for those you have questions about, but even for those you feel great about. Don't be afraid to delay even your best candidates to get a thorough examination of their readiness.

If they are struggling on the field, work with their team leader and missions organization to determine the best course of action. Some missions organizations may provide member care and counseling for missionaries in their country of service. Some missionaries may need to leave the mission field for a season. A few months stateside, or an extended furlough, may refresh and rejuvenate them and allow them to return to the field with a healthier mindset. During this time, consider having them see a third-party counselor in person. A good counselor can pick up on unhealthy patterns and will look for ways to help the missionary take personal responsibility and make necessary changes.

Give your missionaries time to pause. While it may be difficult in the moment and slow the progress of ministry, it is healthier for them long-term.

Getting Started Well

Looking back on my first marathon, I had done everything possible to prepare well. I had coaching, encouragement from friends and family, and all the necessary training. I never thought there would be a storm of that magnitude during my first marathon. I didn't start off well, but by remembering my coaching and my training, I was able to get through the storm and finish the marathon at a personal best time of four hours and five minutes.

Missionaries never start off perfectly. There will always be something unexpected that comes up during that first term. That's the only real expectation you can have! But the sending church can play an important role by giving them a boost and helping them get back on track. You can cheer them on by praying for them and letting them know you are there for them.

The journey for a sending church does not end with commissioning—as we've said, it has only just begun. If your church will take the necessary steps to get your missionaries established, you will not only help them get overseas, but you will help them stay there through the difficulties and challenges they will face. And, by God's grace, you will have the joy of seeing them bear gospel fruit in their lives and ministry.

SENDING CHURCH ELEMENT #12: PROVIDING ONGOING CARE

By Bradley Bell

> **"**
>
> *A sending church provides ongoing care in partnership with a missions organization by building a relational structure that nurtures the health of missionaries for as long as they are sent out. This involves both church leaders and members in advocating holistically for missionaries through prayer, communication, accountability, logistics, visits, and crises.*

"Wilson!"

It's the most famous and endearing line from the film *Castaway* starring Tom Hanks. The story chronicles a man named Chuck Noland whose plane crashes en route to Malaysia and strands him on a deserted island. Severed indefinitely from all relationships, Noland eventually personifies a volleyball as a companion and names him Wilson (since it's already branded on the ball). The two are then inseparable—that is, until Wilson accidentally floats away in the ocean. As Noland fails to rescue him and bawls, "I'm sorry, Wilson!" all the comedy that is left in the situation slowly fades to tragedy.

Indeed, it is no light thing to send people we love to faraway lands. Though such people may be gritty and resilient, no one aside from Christ can fully bear such a cross of separation. They need care. They need relationships. They need to know they are not simply set adrift. And you, the sending church, can give them assurance that they are not forgotten.

A Little Example

Our thinking here isn't just based on modern methodology. We see New Testament glimpses of providing ongoing care, and perhaps no passage is more meaningful than the little letter of 3 John. In this brief correspondence, the apostle John rejoiced that his friend Gaius was "walking in the truth" (v. 3). This was largely evidenced by Gaius's *working* for the truth within his church. How was Gaius working for the truth? In part by *supporting* those sent out to proclaim the truth. We read,

> Beloved, it is a faithful thing you do in all your efforts for these brothers, strangers as they are, who testified to your love before the church. You will do well to send them on their journey in a manner worthy of God. For they have gone out for the sake of the name, accepting nothing from the Gentiles. Therefore we ought to support people like these, that we may be fellow workers for the truth. (3 John 1:5–8)

One of the passage's most remarkable (and easily missed) lines sets the bar for our ongoing care of missionaries: we are to do so "in a manner worthy of God." Consider this: If Jesus himself came to your church and asked you to send him out, how would you do it?

By rolling out the red carpet!

You would be eager to provide him with whatever he needed and support him by any means necessary. It would be a great joy and privilege!

That is the bar. That is the standard John sets for us in all of our ongoing care of the people we send—sending them in a manner worthy of God himself.[1]

A Bigger Vision

Let's be honest, however—many people aren't going to pay much attention to little 3 John. If they do, the obscurity of it may not be enough to motivate a church-wide commitment to missionary care. So consider a bigger vision that has been cosmically displayed before us but strangely left without recognition: missionary care within the Triune God himself.

In some ways, it is a simple activity. Ask yourself and others, "When the Father sent the Son on mission, how did he care for him?" Let me give you a few examples to get your holy imagination flowing:

- » The Father resourced him with his basic needs (Matthew 6:11).
- » The Father was always available to him (Luke 5:16).
- » The Father was so close to him that he could say "he is with me" (John 8:29).
- » The Father gave him the power and presence of the Holy Spirit (Matthew 3:16).
- » The Father verbally affirmed his identity (Matthew 3:17).
- » The Father loved him (John 17:24).
- » The Father sent angels to minister to him (Matthew 4:11; Luke 22:43).
- » The Father allowed him to learn obedience through

suffering instead of pulling him from the field (Hebrews 5:8).

» The Father was willing to rescue him at a word (Matthew 26:53).

» The Father raised him from the dead (Galatians 1:1).

Isn't it a compelling picture of missionary care? There is none better in all of Scripture! Though we cannot fully replicate it (nor do we dare stretch it beyond Trinitarian orthodoxy), we have been shown by God himself what it looks like to care well. This vision could be a powerful motivator for your church to reflect the sending God.

Led by the Church

Setting such a high bar, however, can be intimidating. Perhaps for this reason many churches have relied primarily on missions organizations to provide the ongoing care of those they've sent. After all, such organizations—especially in comparison to local churches—typically have a significant amount of field expertise and personnel. Plus, they are usually receiving overhead from the missionary's support and/or direct donations from local churches, so it's natural to assume that they should, so to speak, do what they've been paid to do.

Although this approach makes sense, it presents a theological difficulty. As we articulated in the prequel to this book, *The Sending Church Defined*, the sending God has placed his sending church at the heart of his global mission. Yes, this means the universal church, including the believers who comprise parachurch ministries. But the universal church is ultimately distilled down to local churches; that is, visible flocks of those transformed by the Chief Shepherd, Jesus Christ, who gather under his authoritative Word and the leadership of his undershepherds.

In regard to such undershepherds, the writer of Hebrews commands, "Obey your leaders and submit to them, for they are keeping watch over your souls, as those who will have to give an account" (Hebrews 13:17). Thus, there is a clear sense of church leaders' ongoing responsibility to care for their flock until a day of accounting to their Chief Shepherd. That means missionary care cannot be fully relinquished.

Supplemented by the Parachurch

Now, to bring some balance, imagine a literal shepherd sending one of his sheep to a far country without personally accompanying it. You don't have to be an agriculturalist to recognize what would happen: that sheep would certainly get lost and likely be devoured in no time! Those who are sent need caring physical presence all along the way. For that reason, we encourage church leaders—who will not be able to provide that abiding presence on the field themselves—to partner well with missions organizations. The key to this is a proper posture of responsibility: ongoing care is to be led by the church and supplemented by the parachurch.

In order for ongoing care to remain the primary responsibility of the church, the church must find missions organizations that support that posture. If both entities see themselves as primary, the missionaries may experience more support for a time, but eventual confusion and possibly even conflict are likely to result. For example, if a missionary is under consideration for a change of assignment and the church and the organization disagree, who makes the final decision? These are complicated matters, and if the two entities are sending divergent messages, the missionary stands to lose the most.

How do you discern a missions organization's posture toward the sending church? In Chapter 6, "Evaluating Sending Models and Partners," we directed you to some helpful questions in this process. Here are a few more specific questions for evaluating their approach to ongoing care:

»   Do they have a doctrinal or convictional statement specifically related to the local church? Does it specify the centrality of the local church in sending?

»   Do they proactively communicate care concerns to church leaders (which may include prior HIPAA clearance)?

»   Have they ever worked with a church that was primarily responsible for providing ongoing care? How did they handle it? Can you speak with a leader from that church to get their perspective?

»   Do they have a member care leader or department? Are they easily accessible to you?

»   What systems and resources do they use for care? What is their on-field infrastructure for care?

»   When care needs arise, will they give you access to your missionaries' field leaders?

»   Do you know anyone who has served within the organization? What was their experience of care like?

Working through detailed questions like these will help you assess organizations, not to find a perfect one, but to discover which ones truly have a high regard for local church involvement. Keep in mind that many missions organizations are still learning about the sending church movement, as they have operated for decades without much interest expressed from local churches. Remembering this will help you be gracious, and perhaps even a source of encouragement, as you partner with a missions organization.

Who Does What?

Another key to care that's "led by the church and supplemented by the parachurch" is determining the specific responsibilities of both entities. In other words, who does what? Ideally, your church and the missions organization will assign and agree upon responsibilities *prior to* the missionary's commissioning. You can foster this by creating a spreadsheet with a detailed list of different care responsibilities. Then add a column for assigning each responsibility to either the sending church, the missions organization, or the missionary. Examples include:

» Who will regularly assess the missionary's mental, physical, social, and spiritual health?
» When counseling is needed, who will provide it?
» Who will be the first responder in crisis care?
» Who will make the final decision on evacuation?
» When a financial need arises beyond the missionary's support, who will assist?
» Who will notify family members during emergency situations?
» Who will provide ongoing accountability?
» Who will give parameters and expectations for the missionary's time off (personal days, sick days, professional development, vacation, furlough, etc.)?
» Who will regularly assess and meet the needs of the children?
» Who will lead in disqualification situations (unrepentant sin, adultery, abuse, embezzlement, heresy, dereliction, etc.)?

If nothing else, having a list like this provides great sobriety in the task of providing ongoing care. And it underscores the need for sending churches to do this in partnership with missions organizations. Few churches have the ability to do it all themselves.

But perhaps the most meaningful effect of the above list is that it should drive the church, the organization, and the missionary into deep relationships with one another. The reality about such responsibilities is that they're not very black and white—it will take involvement from all sides. Like a healthy marriage, mutual trust and open communication will lead to making the best decisions and executing them effectively. Here, the missionary stands to gain the most.

Build a Relational Structure

When the sending church *does* choose to lead the way in providing ongoing care, that care must be built on the foundation of relationships, the kind of relationships that can survive the miles and years of distance between the senders and the sent.

Consider the structure of a skyscraper. Before ever being built up, it must first be built down. In other words, a massive foundation has to be laid. Why? To support the colossal weight of steel and concrete layered high into the sky. Without that foundation, the structure eventually will collapse.

We should realize that the same principle is true in missionary care. It is challenging for a deep, ongoing relationship to be established once the missionary is already sent. Therefore, the foundation for the relationship must be laid long before the commissioning. What does that look like?

The general answer is that it looks like a church with a culture where people can know others and be known. In many sending churches, this involves a commitment to membership and some form of small groups. It does not allow for hiding behind the superficiality of mere church attendance on the way to being sent.

The more specific answer is that it looks like a church with a relational structure that leads up to being sent. Earlier in the book, we described this as a "sending pipeline" (see Chapter 5, "Involving the Entire Church"). The sending pipeline should set a clear expectation for the minimum length of time a candidate is a church member before being sent. Numerous sending churches have set a minimum of around two years—long enough to have established a foundation for the relationship.

Even more importantly, the sending pipeline should be bound up with the interpersonal involvement of church leaders and members. Although it may be tempting to "automate" the process with a series of online forms to complete and boxes to check, nothing can replace a candidate being known and loved at the depth of his or her desires, struggles, and story.

Once that kind of foundation has been laid prior to commissioning, it is much more natural to provide ongoing care in a way that is also relational. And being relational means being reciprocal. When those who have journeyed with a candidate then become part of their ongoing care, it invites not only honesty but also reciprocity. "How are you doing?" and "How can I pray for you?" go both ways between the sender and the sent. This kind of reciprocity gives dignity to the missionary as not simply a recipient but a giver of care as well. That's a true relationship.

Send and Never Let Go

The spirit of this relational structure is captured in a phrase I've often heard from my co-author Nathan Sloan: the church aims to "send and never let go." It is a commitment to nurture the health of those sent for as long as they are sent out. This is easier said than done, especially as the church and missionary change. Thus, accountability systems must be established in addition to the sending covenant (see Chapter 10, "Commissioning Sent Ones"). Below are some of those systems.

Advocate Teams

Advocate teams (also known as "Barnabas" or "missionary care" teams) are small groups of church members (usually four to eight people) who serve as the primary link between the church and the missionary. They carry a dual responsibility. The first is advocating to the church on behalf of the missionary. This means not allowing church leaders or members to forget their commitment to ongoing care. For example, the advocate team may mobilize the church to contribute to a care package or meet a pressing need.

The second responsibility is advocating to the missionary on behalf of the church; that is, being the face of the church at large and communicating important happenings and needs to the missionary. For example, the advocate team may update and involve the missionary in the church's process of hiring a new pastor. This might seem unnecessary, but it goes a long way in giving missionaries an ongoing sense of belonging and participation.

Even more importantly, when an advocate team serves faithfully, their consistent relationship can become a safe space for open and honest communication to take place. Missionaries are more likely to share their successes, failures, strengths, weaknesses, and everything in between when they have a close relationship with the advocate team. And as they relate to church members rather than just leaders, there is less pressure to prove themselves as deserving of the church's support.

Critical to this kind of relationship is the advocates' ability to empathize with the missionaries. Unless advocates have been missionaries themselves, they don't fully understand what missionaries face. But they need to know in order to care well. Enlighten them to what missionaries experience. Describe the highs and lows and the grind. Consider giving them Thomas Hale's *On Being a Missionary*. Better yet, recruit a missionary to give personal testimony.

Realistically, however, an advocate team usually thrives when one participant is recognized as the team leader. This person is responsible for leading meetings, making assignments, and executing plans. If the church has multiple advocate teams for multiple missionaries, it's especially important to have a church leader who oversees and supports the team leaders.

An alternative to this structure is assigning an individual advocate to each missionary unit. If your church has multiple missionaries (and thus multiple advocates), the advocates can meet regularly as an overall missionary care team. This works particularly well in a small church setting.

For a more detailed guide to "Establishing Advocacy Teams," see the Appendix.

Prayer

In addition to the advocate team's regular, specific prayer for the missionary, the entire church body has the privilege and responsibility of faithfully praying for those they send. Hopefully, the expectations for this have been outlined in the sending covenant (once again, see Chapter 10, "Commissioning Missionaries"). For example, the church may have committed to pray "for the missionaries and the people they serve in Sunday services, small groups, households, and the advocate team." If that is the case, the church should then pursue integrity by building rhythms of prayer into these different expressions of church life. To that end, here are some questions to consider:

>> Do we teach that prayer is active participation in God's global mission?

>> How often will we publicly pray for our missionaries and the people they serve in our Sunday services? How do we keep up with that rhythm?

>> How do we practically integrate prayer for our missionaries and the people they serve in our small groups? Who is responsible for coordinating that?

>> What can we do to encourage households to pray? For example, can we provide prayer cards for members to display in their homes?

>> Do we have a mechanism for utilizing specific, time-sensitive prayer requests collected from the advocate team?

>> Are our members encouraged to receive and engage with missionaries' newsletters or social media updates in a way that leads to prayer?

>> Do we occasionally tell stories of answered prayer?

>> If there is already a prayer ministry or group in the

church, has it been mobilized to include prayer for our missionaries and the people they serve?

Logistics

Logistical support is the highly tangible work of meeting everyday felt needs. This support might include managing finances, submitting taxes, providing transportation, supplying housing, storing belongings, buying groceries, etc. It's anything that the missionaries need, especially as they travel between their country of origin and their country of service. In addition to the advocate team's efforts in logistical support, there is a lot the wider church body can do to help as well. In fact, out of all the aspects of missionary care, church members usually feel most naturally inclined to help with logistics. For example, imagine the mutual impact of sending a craftsman team to improve the plumbing, electrical, and structural needs of the missionary's home. That's enough to make anyone feel cared for!

Regarding logistics, here are some questions to ask yourselves:

- » Do we regularly inquire about our missionaries' everyday felt needs?
- » Do we communicate opportunities for logistical support to our members?
- » Do we consider how certain church members (lawyers, doctors, craftsmen, teachers, financial planners, etc.) might assist them?
- » Do we budget to help with our missionaries' logistical needs?
- » Can we empower a person or team to carry this out?

Visits

Missionaries can be deeply encouraged as people come to visit them. Of course, this can take place as a strategic mission trip that supports their ministry. But it can also occur as a "care trip." Care trips have no agenda besides loving the missionaries well. Such visits can allow them to share their life and ministry and enjoy concentrated time with those of their own language and culture. Teams can also serve in other meaningful ways such as paying for nice meals, giving special attention to children, and providing date nights.

Some churches encourage their advocate teams to make visits to their missionaries. This is a hefty responsibility and most likely will require the church leaders' support (although some teams may surprise you with their initiative). The most important factors are that the missionaries actually desire the visit and the time frame, and that the visitors are mature and well-prepared to be a blessing instead of a burden.

Ideally, these visits will also involve church leaders as much as possible. Their presence communicates to the missionaries how valuable they are to the church. In addition, such visits often have a life-changing impact on church leaders, which then directly impacts their ministry in the church. It's a great investment.

Crisis Care

Crisis missionary care can be a daunting undertaking for churches. When a person is sent on mission cross-culturally, it's possible that they could face any of the following: sickness, injury, insufficient medical care, deficient support, war, persecution, theft, threats, sexual assault, natural disaster, kidnapping, torture, imprisonment, terrorism, deportation, civil unrest, mental breakdown, evacuation, witness to crime, major conflict with colleagues, adultery, abandonment, identity loss, job loss, absence from significant family events back home, and even death. However, as Peter admonishes, neither the church nor the missionary should be surprised at such fiery trials (1 Peter 4:12). Although the church may not be prepared for *everything* that could happen, it can at least be prepared that *something* could happen.

This is where it's critical for the sending church to have a relationship with the missions organization. Many organizations have developed policies, systems, and resources for responding to crises, such as contingency training, evacuation plans, travel insurance, and member care. As a first step for churches, it's important to be aware of what the missions organization provides, and perhaps even more importantly, what it *doesn't* provide.

A second step would be finding a contact at the organization in the case of a crisis. For example, when a missionary texts you that they're considering evacuation in light of violent protests in their city, it would be important to consult with an organizational representative before booking the next flight home. In the same way, when an unexpected death occurs in the missionary's family back home, you may want to involve an organizational leader or colleague in the process of communicating the bad news.

A third step would be reading Chapter 15, "Receiving Missionaries during Reentry." Although that chapter is not specifically about crisis care, it does communicate a principle relevant to crisis care: long-term commitment. When churches are present and resourceful at the arrival of a crisis, they function like an emergency room. However, the lasting impact of a crisis often requires more than triage. The wounds may need ongoing care, such as counseling, conflict resolution, or transition. Well-equipped churches will be able to address both the crisis and the trauma it produces.

Accountability

Accountability is necessary, and it's also tricky. Because missionaries represent Jesus Christ and his church among the nations, it's right for them to be held to biblical standards in their character and ministry. At the same time, however, sending churches should seek to maintain ongoing relationships that allow for safety and transparency. How can churches find a balance between having high standards of integrity and offering grace and mercy when missionaries fall short of them?

Part of it begins with setting the right expectations. This is why we advocate for a sending covenant in Chapter 10, "Commissioning Missionaries." This covenant specifies the expectations of both the sending church and the missionary, which then allows for mutual accountability. If the missionary is not living up to the covenant, the church must address it. On the other hand, if the church is not living up to the covenant, then the missionary must address it. Mutuality is important to any relationship.

But beyond that, it's good for the church to determine a relational system for more detailed accountability. We recommend something other than simply having your missionary complete a report (which is likely already required by the missions organization). For example, some churches schedule an annual call with their missionaries during which they talk through predetermined categories of their life and ministry (see the Appendix's "Missionary Health Diagnostic"). Others have a rhythm of monthly calls. Whatever approach you take, communicate your accountability system in advance so that it doesn't come across like a surprise audit. Having this conversation also allows you to ask them if there's anything additional for which they would like accountability.

Serving Well

There are too many stories today of neglected missionaries silently suffering in faraway nations. Even the grittiest and most resilient of Christ-followers need the anchor of ongoing care. You, the sending church, have just what it takes to "send and never let go," to provide relationships of safe harbor and structures for meeting practical needs.

If a church struggles to live up to all the elements of this book but still thrives in providing ongoing care, it will be serving the nations well. Determine now to send in a manner worthy of God and to be fellow workers for the truth with your missionaries by caring for them at every stage in their journey.

SENDING CHURCH ELEMENT #13: MAINTAINING STRATEGIC FOCUS

By Mike Easton

> *A sending church maintains strategic focus by regularly reevaluating the effectiveness of its strategy and ensuring that its responsibilities are not relegated to missions organizations. Missionaries are kept accountable to the church's strategic focus, and partnerships are evaluated for their effectiveness in supporting that focus.*

The rhythms of the calendar are a gift from a good God who created the hearts and rhythms of his children. Each day provides the opportunity to start anew. Each week includes a day of Sabbath rest. Each season brings the end of one routine and the start of a new one. Each new year is a milestone by which we can remember the past and look forward to what's to come.

These rhythms allow us to rest, remember, and reflect. We know from the Old Testament that God instituted feasts—the biblical equivalent of holidays—that would take place multiple times each year (Exodus 23:14) and provide opportunities to rejoice and celebrate God's faithfulness (Leviticus 23:40; Deuteronomy

16:14; Nehemiah 8:17).

God's consistent command to remember his works (twenty-five times in the Old Testament) still has relevance today, even for the sending church. Pausing to reflect actually has a deep connection with moving wisely toward the future. In this element we will encourage you at this stage in sending to make a practice of reevaluation at this stage in the sending rather than simply barreling ahead. This will help keep you on course.

Mission Drift

On November 28, 1979, a DC-10 airplane flying a sightseeing group from New Zealand crashed into Mount Erebus on Ross Island, Antarctica. The crash killed all 257 passengers on board. In the followup investigation it was determined that the flight path in the plane's computer was off by two degrees, which ultimately led them twenty-eight miles off course. A mere two-degree drift became a total disaster.[1]

Thankfully, sending churches aren't in the business of flying airplanes! But a similar kind of drift *is* possible. This is often referred to as "mission drift," a slow move away from our original intended purpose and identity. In their book on the topic, Peter Greer and Chris Horst give examples of organizations that were once gospel-centered but slowly embraced a different vision and mission, such as Harvard, Yale, and the YMCA.[2] Other common expressions of mission drift include denominations that have lost their Christ-centered vision, churches that have stopped reaching out to their community with the gospel, and missionaries that only leave their house for necessities. Like the airplane mentioned above, we're all susceptible to veering off course—often without even realizing it.

As a follower of Christ and a leader in ministry, one of my favorite scriptures for recalibrating my life is 1 Corinthians 3:10–15. There Paul describes Christ as the foundation of the church and gives a warning to anyone who labors in the church. He says, "each one is to be careful how he builds on it" (v. 10), because one day our work will be tested by fire. Only that which God approves will endure and be rewarded. The rest will be burned up.

While this is one of my favorite scriptures, it is also one of the scariest to me. There is so much that can take us off course: our cultural norms, our worldview, the critics around us, the inner critic, our self-centeredness. All of these can cause mission drift. In addition to our regular times with the Lord in study and prayer, we need seasonal blocks of time to recalibrate ourselves to the ministry vision God has for us.

Evaluating Oneself as a Missions Leader

Leadership requires self-evaluation. 1 Peter 5:1–5 reminds us that a leader must be a servant-hearted shepherd, not one wielding authority for their own desires. We all know Christian leaders who, while well-intended, have allowed their insecurity, tendency toward people-pleasing, and desire for control to subtly cloud their judgment. If it's possible for others to do, it's possible for you and me to do as well.

Therefore, before evaluating others, as leaders we must start with evaluating ourselves—our motives, rhythms, and practices. If we're not characterized by self-awareness, we are not prepared to help others be self-aware. This means, with God's help, attuning to the needs of our soul, family, and ministry. We need this as much as our missionaries do.

Here are some personal reflections to consider to evaluate yourself as a missions leader:

>> Is my soul healthy? My family? My ministry?
>> What can I celebrate from this past year?
>> What has been burdensome or stressful this past

year?

» What were some of my driving motives?

» What did I carry that I no longer need to?

» What did I fail to carry that I now need to pick up?

» Do I have helpful rhythms and boundaries?

» Are my priorities flowing from our vision and strategy?

Fellow missions leaders, remember that out of the overflow of the heart, the mouth speaks (Luke 6:45). Remember that we can do nothing apart from our Savior (John 15:4–5). Take time for personal reflection, evaluation, and recalibration for your sake and for the sake of those you serve.

Evaluating Your Strategy as a Sending Church

After you've given some attention to your own health, you can begin to evaluate your church. The vision and strategy document you created in Chapters 3 and 4 will help you do this. In that document you outlined what you hope to see exhibited in the lives and ministry of your missionaries. It is important to regularly evaluate this document to tweak your vision and strategy. Opportunities and threats on the mission field will arise and will require a response. Your church's vision will grow and shift. It will change in size, budget, and demographics. Your missions vision and strategy will need to adapt to these changes.

The following are some questions to consider in this process:

» What changes have we seen in our church and on the mission field since we last evaluated our missions vision and strategy?

» Are there any new partners we've connected with whose vision should shape our vision?

» Are there any existing partners that no longer fit in our vision?

» How should we change our existing budget to reflect

our changes in strategy?

» What missiological resources should we be studying that can help further shape our strategy as a church?

Evaluating Your Mobilization

As you ask these questions and make changes, it will likely also impact your approach to mobilization. For example, if what you want to accomplish on the field has shifted, then you'll need to be preparing missionary candidates to fit into the revised strategy. Furthermore, what worked in mobilization when your church was small may not work if your church has grown significantly. A smaller church can be more informal in mobilization. A larger church needs to think more systematically about that process. A church's size will absolutely impact the missions vision and scope and the way they relate to sending.[3]

Some questions for evaluating your mobilization strategy could include:

» What characteristics are missing from our missionaries who are already on the field? How can we better develop those qualities in our missionary candidates?

» What isn't being accomplished on the field? Who needs to be sent to fill the gap?

» Does our growth in sending mean that we need to formalize more of our sending processes?

» Has our church changed in ways that necessitate more effective forms of mobilization?

Evaluating Your Missionaries

In the previous chapter, we discussed the importance of providing ongoing care. Caring for your missionaries' souls is absolutely essential. However, you haven't sent church members solely to live a healthy vertical life with God overseas. You have also sent them to be fruitful in the horizontal mission of proclaiming the gospel in word and deed. While it is important and primary to evaluate how they are doing personally, it is also important to evaluate how they are fulfilling the vision and strategy of their work. This is both a loving act and faithful stewardship.

The evaluation of a missionary is a delicate process. There are many factors at play for the person. Their role is professional, but it's also very personal. For many, their identity is wrapped up in the work. Understandably so! They have moved their family overseas, given up another career, and in many cases raised support to do their work. There is no 9-to-5 in missionary life. All the more reason to give careful thought to how you evaluate.

The old adage "It's not what you said, it's how you said it" is a helpful reminder here. Considering not only the "what" but also the "how" in our evaluation increases the likelihood of its effectiveness. Ellen Livingood gives some helpful tips for having evaluations that strengthen the missionary rather than demoralize them. She begins with four missteps.

1. A report instead of a relationship: An annual evaluation should not be done if it is the only point of contact between the church and the missionary.
2. Busywork: The questions must be unique, not simply restating what they have already shared in one-on-one or other meetings.
3. Hidden expectations: Be clear that the goal of the evaluation is forward movement, not to find fault with or critique the individual.
4. A report instead of an evaluation: Evaluations have dialogue; reports do not. Create space for a dialogue, not simply an inventory report.

On the other hand, Livingood continues, there are five ways to foster trust in the process. They include:

1. A safe environment: Be clear about who will see the evaluation.
2. Celebration: Make the evaluation's main goal to celebrate and praise the Lord for what he has done in and through your missionary.
3. Finding gaps: Not everything comes up in natural conversation or one-on-ones. Evaluations create space to find areas of concern that may have slipped through the cracks.
4. Partnership course corrections: Partnerships need to be evaluated. If the supervisory structure of your missionary is unhealthy, then you need to create space for them to give you feedback.
5. Looking forward more than back: As the missionary works in an ever-changing landscape, it is important for the sending church to understand these changes and be on the same page about what's next.[4]

In addition to these suggestions, having a vision and strategy document specifically for the missionary is a great reference point for the evaluation. This is likely an exercise that the missionary will do with their missions organization. If they have not, however, you can refer to the basic principles from Chapters 3 and 4 to help them create and develop that document. Then you can use it as a recalibration tool.

We also encourage you to create your own evaluation based on your vision, values, and strategy for your missionary. Focus on questions that get them to think about their relationship with God, their family, and other important relationships. Also include questions that help them celebrate the past before looking to improve in the future. If you need an example from which to draw, see the Appendix for a "Simple Annual Review of a Missionary from a Sending Church Template" and "Strategic Reflection Questions Missionaries Should Ask."

Continue, Stop, Start

The healthy evaluation of missionaries often leads them to address their own strategic approach to ministry. A great framework for fostering this is using the headings "continue," "stop," and "start." Each heading serves as a category of questions, which can allow the missionary to immediately turn their reflections into applications for the next year or term. It looks something like this.

Continue: What has been a wise use of the missionary's time that they should continue to do? Beginning here is a great way to encourage the missionary and to keep prioritizing certain endeavors and objectives. Some supporting questions could include:

>> With the vision and strategy of your ministry in mind, what are key aspects that have been executed faithfully?
>> Have these been fruitful?
>> What aspects of the ministry have been executed with faithfulness but have not yet borne fruit?

Stop: What is the missionary doing that they should discontinue? Some supporting questions could include:

>> Is there anything you are doing that is not what you must do?
>> Is there anything you are doing for the missions organization or partner that is unnecessary or unprofitable?
>> Is there anything you are spending a lot of time on that isn't in your job description or a part of the strategy?

Start: What has the missionary not been doing that they should start? What are new objectives that they need to work toward accomplishing? Some supporting questions could include:

>> Are there aspects of the vision and strategy you are

not making an effort towards?

» In light of this, what should you start doing that you have not been doing?

» Is there an opportunity for ministry or a threat to existing ministry that warrants starting a new project or endeavor?

As you go through this exercise, be sure to encourage your missionaries. Listen to them. Listen to their challenges. Your job in this situation is not to provide all the answers for them but to help them ask and answer reflective questions they may not be asking in their normal rhythm.

Some missions leaders are great at caring for and connecting with people but struggle with this kind of evaluative process. If working through strategy with your missionaries seems impossible, don't be afraid to lean on others to help you. Look to your church's executive pastor, a counselor, a business person, or a consulting organization for help. Such resources can help you be effective as you help your missionaries be effective.

Evaluating the On-Field Partner and Missions Organization

As we discussed in Chapter 6, "Evaluating Sending Pathways and Partners," the missions organization and on-field supervisor are pivotal partners in sending strategically. Their decisions and actions directly impact the missionary's overall experience. What vital services are they providing? Are they executing their roles in a helpful way? Are they creating unnecessary work for your missionaries? It's wise to regularly evaluate them in this way.

Maintaining a relationship with on-field partners and missions organizations is what will allow you to make this evaluation holistically. These partners are people too, and so evaluating them isn't simply about reports and numbers. When they are fulfilling their roles well, it is worthy of celebration and affirmation.

At the same time, just because such partnerships have worked in the past doesn't mean they have to last for a lifetime. Even when your church and the missions organization don't see eye to eye, your relationship with them is likely more of a tension to manage than a problem to solve. You will always be tweaking aspects of how the missions organization relates to your missionaries, and breaking a working relationship with a missions organization is a big step and not something you would want to take lightly (not to mention something that would deeply impact your missionaries). However, if the missions organization begins to hinder the ministry of the missionaries and your intention as a sending church, don't be afraid to make the hard decision of making a change.

Practically speaking, a key way to evaluate your on-field partners and missions organizations is by hearing the perspective of your missionaries. They have the tangible, ongoing experience of how these partners actually function. To this end, some questions you could ask your missionaries include:

- » What do you like about your missions organization and team?
- » Are there any unhealthy organizational or team issues we should know about?
- » How is your team helping you to be on mission and live life in a healthy way?
- » Are you being encouraged to serve not only according to the vision and strategy but also your giftings?
- » Are you experiencing responsibilities or dynamics that are counterproductive?

A Church in Practice

Some years ago, a church I was consulting with underwent a significant process of reevaluating their vision, partnerships, and budget. The evaluative process began with their missions team noticing gaps in their missions vision and where they believed God wanted them to be. They spent time talking with missionaries, their missions team, elder team, and getting consulting from outside groups like Upstream. They reworked their vision and strategy. Then they reworked their budget based on that. They took on the task of having their leadership team come to an agreement on the principles. And finally, they communicated in person or through video to their members and their missionaries the reason for the changes and the vision moving forward.

Because they took the time to do this with wisdom and intentionality, they came out of that season without any major difficulty. No missionary likes having sudden changes thrust upon them, but because the decision was carefully considered and communicated, they could look back with satisfaction on the relationship they had with the church rather than with bitterness about how they were treated. Church members weren't blindsided by the changes because they understood the "why" behind each decision. Most importantly, the vision and strategy were clearer to the church and reflected rightly in their budget.

This kind of maintenance to the strategy may not be the most exciting of the Sending Church Elements, but it could be the most important for the longevity of healthy sending. And as the church above has shown, it is possible to do it in a way that synergizes everyone involved.

A Pivotal Role

Following the tragic plane crash of 1979, it was determined that, while there was some fault on the part of the pilots, the airline was also to blame for allowing the plane to fly below recommended altitudes. The lack of attention to strategic guidelines didn't seem to matter much—until it exacted the highest price.

As a sending church, we can help our people stay on course, out of danger, and in the lane God is calling them to run in. Doing so can involve hard conversations, persistence, and courage, no doubt. Maintaining strategic guidelines may even feel like wasted energy amidst the demands of so many other things. But in the end, through consistent and careful evaluation of ourselves, our strategy, our missionaries, and our partners, we can play a pivotal role in helping them be faithful to live out the mission to which they have been called.

PART 4: MULTIPLYING PHASE

The church matures in its sending ability and influence.

In Chapters 10 to 13, we focused on the "Engaging" phase of the Sending Church Elements and how the church supports the missionary as they begin ministering to people with the gospel cross-culturally.

As your church matures in sending, you will need to consider the "Multiplying" phase of the Sending Church Elements. This phase comes into play as your missionaries gain some time and experience on the field. Element #14 focuses on how to invite your missionaries' influence back on the sending church. Element #15 speaks to the critical responsibility of caring for missionaries during reentry. Element #16 challenges you to be thinking ahead, innovating as the world of missions changes. And Element# 17 guides you in the most exponential way to be fruitful as a sending church: by influencing other churches.

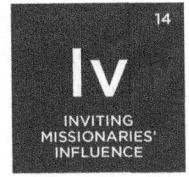

SENDING CHURCH ELEMENT #14: INVITING MISSIONARIES' INFLUENCE

By Bradley Bell

66

A sending church invites missionaries' influence when it eagerly desires the unique encouragement that comes from missionaries, as modeled in the New Testament. Whether the missionaries are on the field or on furlough, the church initiates opportunities for them to influence through presence, reporting, and exhortation.

It's a well-known story to basketball fans that Michael Jordan, arguably the greatest basketball player of all time, didn't make the varsity team as a high school sophomore. Instead, he had to settle for the junior varsity, where he often scored forty points per game. Sure, he was young and physically underdeveloped. But just imagine how his team missed out on a gold mine of potential! The player who would go on to be the star of collegiate and professional basketball was, at first, one of the greatest untapped resources of all time. It's almost unbelievable.

The unfortunate parallel is that missionaries are often one of the greatest untapped resources in the local church. Churches can easily release them to the nations, entrusting them to the care of missions organizations and relegating them solely to another context. Their ministry is considered "over there," which often assumes the conclusion of their ministry "over here." Settling for this false binary, then, means that the missionaries become "junior varsity" in terms of their influence on churches. As a result, we effectively miss out on the gold mine of their passion, wisdom, sacrifice, skills, gifts, struggles, and missiology. It, too, is almost unbelievable.

A New Testament Vision

Once again, we are going to give our attention to the sending church at Antioch. Certainly, this was an age in which long-distance communication was challenging, if not impossible. If any church were to have a justifiable reason for releasing their missionaries to the nations and relegating them solely to another context, Antioch could have made a good case for it. But something surprising occurred at the conclusion of Paul and Barnabas's journey. We read in Acts 14:24–28,

> Then they passed through Pisidia and came to Pamphylia. And when they had spoken the word in Perga, they went down to Attalia, and from there they sailed to Antioch, where they had been commended to the grace of God for the work that they had fulfilled. And when they arrived and gathered the church together, they declared all that God had done with them, and how he had opened a door of faith to the Gentiles. And they remained no little time with the disciples.

Even though this is only a passing glimpse into the return of Paul and Barnabas, there are a number of things we can learn from it.

Place Matters

Luke lists a number of cities without description in verses 24 and 25, but notice the emphasis he gives to Antioch: "where they had been commended to the grace of God for the work that they had fulfilled." Antioch was a meaningful place, not merely geographically, but spiritually and narratively as well. The sending church was there, and something sacred happened there. Something started there, so it was natural to finish there. In a clear sense, Paul and Barnabas had come home.

Publicity Matters

Because a wider group of people had participated in the sending phenomenon (see Chapter 5, "Involving the Entire Church," and Chapter 10, "Commissioning Missionaries"), keeping the journey's results private would have been inappropriate. Going public also provided an opportunity to declare God's praises and works among the nations (see Psalm 96:2–3), a task Paul and Barnabas were sure not to miss. Thus they "gathered the church together [and] declared all that God had done with them."

Presence Matters

Perhaps the most striking and mysterious description of Paul and Barnabas's return to Antioch is that "they remained no little time with the disciples." What does that mean, and why was it necessary to include? Simply put, it was necessary because presence matters. They stayed a long time with their beloved brothers and sisters at Antioch. Consider this: Paul and Barnabas hadn't just been sent; they had also experienced things like:

- » Being world travelers and cross-cultural navigators
- » Being disappointed with a teammate (John Mark, who abandoned them)
- » Being performers of miracles

- » Being run out of towns
- » Being stoned nearly to death
- » Being worshiped as gods (to their horror)
- » Being church planters everywhere they went
- » Being on the front row as the gospel advanced among the Gentiles

It would have been impossible to unpack all those experiences in one meeting! That's not to mention all the reentry soul care they may have needed. The greatest gift they could have given—and received—was to remain among the church, not simply to report and move on. Their time together was prolonged because it needed to be.

All that to say, imagine the influence that came from honoring the place, publicizing the journey, and offering their presence. Let your imagination be stirred, not with a picture of Paul and Barnabas boring people to tears in an endless public gathering, but of them talking with friends over meals and long walks and household chores. Consider the impact of people encountering not just the soaring gifts of these leaders but also the humanity of their struggles and imperfections. It would've been deeply edifying.

Recognizing the Gold

To be compelled by this New Testament vision, then, is to recognize the unique encouragement that comes from those sent out on mission. Wise church leaders say, "There's a gold mine here!" They see it as divinely woven into the very calling and identity of a missionary, especially missionaries who have a deep affection for the local church.

Consider Paul's life and ministry. We look to him as the prime example of a cross-cultural missionary. Yet his life was a "helix" of both ministry to the nations *and* ministry to the local church. Use this graphic to consider the parallels in his story:

Paul's Ministry to the Church	Paul's Ministry to the Nations
Converted among the church - Acts 9:19	Called as an apostle to Gentiles - Acts 9:15
Pastored at Antioch - Acts 11:26	Sent out from Antioch - Acts 13:3
Returned to Antioch - Acts 14:26	Sent out from Antioch - Acts 15:2
Returned to Antioch - Acts 15:35	Sent out from Antioch - Acts 15:40

Paul's ministry to the church and his ministry to the nations are so intertwined throughout his story that it's almost unhelpful to distinguish between them. Only a cursory glimpse into his life speaks to the mutual relationship between the sender and the sent. I like to summarize my observation like this: just as the church continually initiates love (Philippians 4:10), prayer (Ephesians 6:18–19), and resources (Romans 15:24) to the missionary, the missionary continually initiates love (Philippians 1:4), prayer (Ephesians 1:16), and resources (Colossians 4:7–9) to the church.

Yet this is still not quite strong enough to capture Paul's relationships with churches. Rarely do we see him merely reciprocating. Rather, his *initiating* affection for those churches is written all over his missionary identity. We find him writing heartfelt letters to them (2 Corinthians 2:4), agonizing over their lack of growth (Galatians 4:19–20), praying for them constantly (1 Thessalonians 1:2), being delighted to spend time with them (Romans 15:23–24), wooing them to join in the mission (Philippians 1:27–30), avoiding being a financial burden to them (2 Thessalonians 3:7–8), rejoicing over them (1 Thessalonians 2:17–20), and weeping with them (Acts 20:36–38).

For all that Paul embodies as one changed by God and obedient in his mission, he also showcases an appropriate missionary posture toward the church in word and deed. Was he so driven in his relationship with local churches because he was a highly gifted apostle? Was it merely his responsibility to act this way as one who *established* many of those churches? Did he initiate only because he had the *authority* to do so? Theologian George W. Peters argues against this line of thinking when he writes, "Paul did not exercise such authority in missionary partnership. Here he was a humble brother and energetic leader among fellow laborers, and a dynamic and exemplary force in the churches in evangelism and church expansion."[1]

No doubt Paul's frontier dreams were "slowed down" due to his sometimes inconvenient devotion to local churches. He experienced neglect and discouragement from churches (see Philippians 4:10–15; Galatians 1:4; Acts 21:13; 2 Corinthians 2:1–4). He carried an overwhelming ministry load (see 2 Corinthians 11:28). He could have chosen to operate exclusively within a mobile missionary team.

But he didn't.

Despite every failure and hindrance, Paul *loved* the church (see Philippians 4:1; 1 Thessalonians 2:8). He knew that abandoning the bride of Christ meant insulting her groom, Christ himself. He knew the church, with all her warts, was neither an inconvenience nor a side note to the mission of God.

Now imagine if your church's missionaries took the same posture. Pure gold!

Mining the Gold before They're Sent

Recognizing this kind of potential is an important first step, but how do you tap into it? The reality is, most missionaries will not naturally have this perspective. Though they love the local church, their eyes are most compelled toward the nations. They are often simply living in the false binary of local versus global ministry that we ourselves have fostered. It is up to the sending church, then, to cultivate the same posture in them that we see in Paul.

Ideally, this begins long before missionaries are sent. Missions leaders proactively give them a vision for continuing to have an impact on the local church through an ongoing, reciprocal relationship. It helps them to see their inherent potential to have a fruitful ministry both "over there" and "over here." There are a few practical ways to achieve this.

Involve Missionary Candidates in Missionary Care

Involving them in care allows them to experience (often for the first time) what it means to have a fruitful ministry both "over here" and "over there." As they are rooted on this side of the world, they get a feel for what it means to be "fellow workers for the truth" (3 John 1:8) while simultaneously contributing to ministry on the other side of the world. It *is* possible!

Cast Vision in Pre-Field Training

If you have any classes or trainings as part of your sending pipeline (see Chapter 9, "Developing Missionaries"), devote a session to the potential influence of missionaries. Saturate participants in the examples of Acts 14 and Paul's helix of ministry among the churches and the nations. Articulate the church's desire to benefit from the gold mine of their passion, wisdom, sacrifice, skills, gifts, struggles, and missiology. Explain to them the eternal value of making room in their ministries to initiate love, prayer, and resources back in the direction of the sending church.

Give Them Examples

Put the principle to the test by letting existing missionaries influence potential missionaries. Ask existing missionaries to describe why and how they go about influencing the church. Have them give examples of fruit that has come from their efforts. As a former missionary, I love telling stories of how I went about this, which included:

- » Writing regular, thoughtful, honest, readable, photo-filled updates
- » Sharing specific prayer needs, asking for church members' specific prayer needs, and praying for them
- » Making care package needs known for myself and my team
- » Sending encouraging hand-written letters to the church
- » Corresponding with children's classes
- » Shooting videos for the church to use
- » Sending strategic care packages to the church, including gifts and cultural items to display
- » Offering to coordinate and receive short-term teams and mid-term teammates
- » Initiating friendly communication simply to maintain relationships
- » Sharing my struggles to deconstruct the missionary pedestal

The best part about telling my stories is getting to share about the fruit that came from my efforts. Only heaven will reveal the full results of this investment, but here's what I know:

- » Numerous people sensed a calling to be sent through the influence of my updates.
- » I once received nine care packages in one day (that has to be a record!).
- » Many church members became "fellow workers for the truth" through praying strategically and giving financially.
- » One college student became a mid-term teammate.
- » Eventually, I joined Upstream, where I get to share these examples with churches and missionaries all over the world.

What a joy to have had this kind of influence back in my home culture! And especially so in my sending and supporting churches.

Mining the Gold after They're Sent

All the above can take place *before* a missionary is even sent. But how can you be proactive to glean their influence *after* they have been commissioned? In other words, how can you initiate opportunities to make it *easy* for them to influence the church? Three categories come to mind.

Presence

One way to have missionaries' influence is simply to give the expectation that you'd like them to "remain no little time with the disciples" (Acts 14:28). That is, you'd like for them to commit a certain amount of their furloughs and visits to being present with the church—and not just physically present, but relationally engaged as well. Participating in Sunday services and joining a small group is a good place to start.

This also means giving the expectation that you'd like them to make themselves available for receiving occasional field visits. Of course, you will need to consider what capacity they have for hosting visitors, but welcoming church leaders and members into their life and ministry can be a short-term investment with a long-term impact. In terms of influence, nothing quite compares to the gift of a missionary's personal presence (see Romans 1:11–12 and Acts 20:36–38).

Finally, work to invite their presence by updating them on the church's life. Make them aware of secure avenues by which they can remain knowledgeable of the church's vision, activities, and changes. For example, you can invite them to participate in a staff meeting (whether virtually or in person) in which you share about major happenings, such as changes in leadership or launching a new service. Invite their feedback if they have any. At the very least, including them in this way will open your church to the influence of their prayers.

Reporting

Another way to make it easy for missionaries to influence the church is by giving them multiple avenues to "declare all that God has done with them" (Acts 14:27). No doubt this brings to mind the idea of giving them stage time at a Sunday service (as much as possible!). But this can also include having them speak at special gatherings such as receptions, potlucks, and prayer meetings. Also help them schedule times to share in smaller settings such as Sunday School classes, small groups, children and student groups, staff meetings, etc. As you do, give them clarity and guidelines on how to share most effectively (length of time, context of setting, desired outcome, etc.).

You can also open the door for missionaries to report while they're still overseas. Thanks to today's technology, there are lots of ways to do this (although the occasional handwritten letter is actually a powerful ancient Christian practice!). Where security allows, consider things like:

>> Inviting them to report at a gathering via live feed
>> Asking them to record a video report
>> Having them send a voice memo report
>> Assigning someone (ideally an advocate) to report on their behalf
>> Requesting they write short stories that can be told and/or posted online
>> Encouraging them to send photos that could be displayed as an art gallery

Get creative! It's fun, and it's worth the effort to help your missionaries influence the church through reporting.

Exhortation

A final category to proactively pursue is exhortation; that is, missionaries making urgent appeals to the church. We often do not expect more from missionaries than sending in reports, but they have much more to offer! Consider Paul and Barnabas being sent to represent Antioch at the Jerusalem Council in Acts 15, then returning to report the good news. There we read, "Paul and Barnabas remained in Antioch, teaching and preaching the word of the Lord, with many others also" (Acts 15:35). The church was nourished by their exhortation.

However, exhorting the church in this way does not come naturally to most missionaries. Out of respect for their church leaders' authority, and with perhaps a lack of vision for a local *and* global ministry, they tend to hold back all that may be in their hearts to say. Let them know that their exhortation—as rooted in Scripture and tempered by the Spirit (not guided by cultural frustration)—is of great value to the church and that you desire it. Then give them an easy way to deliver it, such as:

> » During a commissioning or report, include the interview question "Do you have a word of exhortation for us?"
> » Ask them to write a letter of encouragement and exhortation to the church that you will read publicly.
> » If a missionary has the gift and desire to preach, provide the opportunity for them to do so.
> » If a missionary has a national partner with a word of exhortation for the church, welcome it.

Missions leaders can sometimes grow weary of making the same urgent appeals to their congregation and seeing little to no progress. It may be that when the same exhortation comes from a missionary, movement finally begins to happen. So don't miss out! Take advantage of this rare form of influence.

For a practical summary of these steps, see the Appendix's "Inviting a Missionary's Influence in Your Church." And you might consider giving the guide "Influencing Your Sending Church" to your missionaries for their own application (also found in the Appendix).

Go for Gold

Cultivating a healthy sending church is certainly too great a burden for a single leader. An ideal way to lighten your load and multiply your effort is by inviting missionaries' influence. Like Michael Jordan playing junior varsity, missionaries are an untapped resource, an absolute gold mine of potential missions impact. When they have a deep affection for the church and are given avenues to express what God is doing in and through them, it will bring rich edification. And they will expand their ministry not just to "over there" but also "over here," giving them the joy of blessing their sending church.

So you do well to recognize this gold and mine it. It will be for your good, their good, and the good of the church.

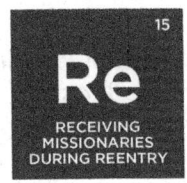

RECEIVING
MISSIONARIES
DURING REENTRY

SENDING CHURCH ELEMENT #15:
RECEIVING MISSIONARIES DURING REENTRY

By Bradley Bell

> *A sending church receives missionaries during reentry by planning to meet their missionaries' needs (including those of their children) when they return on furlough, transition indefinitely, or retire. Aware of the unique challenges of reentry, church leaders and members give special attention to debriefing and ongoing care. They also seek to help missionaries assimilate back into culture and reintegrate into the church's local mission.*

Paul Bäumer was a ghost when he left the trenches of World War I. Returning to his family and town, which had changed little, he was welcomed back as the same beloved boy who'd grown up there. But he was no longer that boy.

"I breathe deeply," Bäumer reflects, "and say over to myself: 'You are at home; you are at home.' But a sense of strangeness will not leave me, I can find nothing of myself in all these things. There is my mother, there is my sister, there is my case of butterflies, and there is the mahogany piano—but I am not myself there. There is a distance, a veil between us."[1]

Although Bäumer is a fictional character in Erich Maria Remarque's famous novel *All Quiet on the Western Front*, his experience of being in the physical presence of loved ones and yet not really being seen or known is haunting. While missionaries are not soldiers, they are similarly changed in profound ways that are hard for others to understand. Returning to their culture of origin, then, like Bäumer, can be no less ghostly and painful.

What Is a Returning Missionary?

A returning missionary is a cross-cultural worker who temporarily or indefinitely reenters his or her culture of origin. The possible categories for such a return include furlough, transition, and retirement. Although these categories are straightforward, the underlying reasons for returns are numerous and complex. They may include the need for rest, financial support, healthcare, conflict resolution, family visits, children's resources, or coming to terms with things like culture shock, trauma, or moral failure.

Years ago, I was one of those returning missionaries. I had come back to marry my fiancée. We planned to be in the U.S. for one year and then return to my former country of service as career missionaries. Over the course of that year, however, I realized that dream would not materialize. I suddenly felt like a ghost. I was home, but home wasn't home anymore. I was Bradley, but Bradley wasn't Bradley anymore. All these years later, I still feel it sometimes.

The pain points of a missionary in reentry are profuse—too many to account for and too specific to generalize here. But as a pastor and friend to many returning missionaries, I've observed a common thread that makes their collective griefs profoundly worse: no one really understands. And if they were honest, I think many missionaries would say that few people seem to really care.

What Is the Role of the Sending Church?

The local church is meant to be a harbor from which missionaries can set sail on their journeys abroad. As we have described throughout this book, with some intentionality, the local church can be the central sender and sustainer of its missionaries. We are introduced to this vision through the church at Antioch, which in obedience to the Holy Spirit, sent Barnabas and Saul (see Acts 13:1–3). But those two great missionaries also returned to the believers in Antioch, where they both served and were served by their home church (see Acts 14:24–28; 15:35; 18:22). Thus, we see that a sending church is also meant to be a safe harbor to which missionaries can return.

Unfortunately, many churches don't know how to do this well. We reveal our ignorance when we ask returning missionaries questions like, "So how was your trip?" and "Aren't you so glad to be home?" We mean well. But imagine the insensitivity experienced by missionaries who have rooted their lives overseas, people for whom "home" has come to mean "elsewhere" or "nowhere." Our failure to ask deeper questions and truly listen doesn't make the harbor unsafe, just inhospitable. The returnee quietly feels like a ghost in a gospel environment. Somehow, the hospitality he or she received from non-Christians overseas becomes more meaningful than that of their home church in their own culture.

The Ugly Duckling of Sending

When soldiers leave the front lines, they come back changed. We are only now beginning to understand the true depth of wartime wounds. Most civilians have no categories of similar experience, no language to empathize, and no capacity to respond. There's nothing glorious about rehabbing prosthetics, replacing bandages, or weathering PTSD outbursts. Similarly, when men, women, and children sent to the mission field's front come back weary and hurting, it can be challenging to offer more than encouraging words. Receiving missionaries during reentry might well be called "the ugly duckling" of the sending process because, simply put, it's much easier to send people out than to receive them back.

Being sent doesn't always mean signing up for death, but it does guarantee a series of small deaths. Kelly O'Donnell writes, "From the day one enters the process of becoming a missionary, spiritual, emotional, interpersonal, and physical stresses begin to multiply, and these stresses usually continue unabated throughout one's career."[2] Sarah Hay points to a study that shows 40 percent of cross-cultural workers develop a psychological disorder, such as depression, while on the field or shortly after returning home.[3] These disorders manifest upon return because the collective wounds they've received from life and ministry overseas are then magnified by the returning missionary's greatest enemy: reverse culture shock.

Reverse Culture Shock

After all the adjustments required from learning a new language and culture, reentering one's former home can cause as much or more stress than going to the field.[4] In her book *Burn Up or Splash Down*, Marion Knell uses the analogy of a spaceship reentering Earth's atmosphere to parallel reverse culture shock, but says it's ultimately more like being an alien on a flying saucer.[5] This transition is the most difficult for children, or "TCKs" (Third Culture Kids), because reentry is more like entry, as they've often only known life elsewhere.[6]

This experience commonly includes prolonged feelings of surprise, disorientation, confusion, frustration, boredom, cynicism, and alienation, which then extend into the rollercoaster stages of excitement, withdrawal, hostility, and readjustment. The degree to which they experience these emotions often corresponds with their reason for returning: furlough, transition, or retirement.

Furlough

As intentional, temporary returns from the field, furloughs can be sacred seasons for missionaries. They are intended to provide time and distance for things such as resting, renewing contact with the church and family, raising funds, recruiting workers, reporting on the ministry, reintroducing children to their country of origin, and refreshing training.[7] Yet sometimes, furloughs can be counterproductive. Imagine trying to accomplish all the above tasks in only a few months—*while experiencing reverse culture shock*. The combination of busyness and cultural readjustment can cause many missionaries to return overseas just as fatigued as when they left.

Transition

"Transition" is a catch-all for any reason that a missionary indefinitely returns from the field. Such returns can stem from positive circumstances, such as a sense of God's leadership, a change of assignment, or completion of the work (which was Paul and Barnabas's conclusion in Acts 14:26). However, they often result from negative circumstances or experiences on the field. Sadly, this can include things like unresolved team conflict, expulsion, incurable sickness, or emotional trauma.

Because of our tendency to put missionaries on a pedestal, we can struggle to have a category for them when they return sooner than we expected. So, in addition to their own experience of loss, missionaries in transition also may grapple with a sense of failure in the eyes of others. This is not to mention the added stress of changing careers. As you can imagine, the reverse culture shock for these returning missionaries is quickly magnified.

Retirement

Retirement is a seldom-considered stage in a missionary's life, and yet it could be the most challenging. Bidding farewell to the field can be as hard for a long-term missionary as giving up the car keys is for an ailing parent. Returning after so many years abroad can lead to a severe identity crisis, which can be compounded by the grief of final goodbyes, looming health concerns, and lack of financial preparation for retirement. Additionally, churches have likely changed just as much as the retirees over the years, leaving the former missionaries feeling perpetually out of place and underutilized. At its worst, retirement could mean facing seemingly unending waves of reverse culture shock.

Planning, Presence, Provision

Of course, not all aspects of returning are so gloomy, and God is faithful to minister to missionaries according to their unique needs. How can the sending church participate with God in that ministry? How can it be a safe harbor for those who need to be resupplied and sent back, or rehabbed and kept home? Consider three key steps: planning, presence, and provision.

Planning

First of all, churches need to think ahead. Don't wait until those you've sent arrive back home. Hopefully, you've remained in a close enough relationship with them that you know in advance when they plan to return (see Chapter 12, "Providing Ongoing Care"). Having a few months' notice allows you to begin making a plan for receiving them. This plan begins with the simple question, "What do you need?" Knowing their needs keeps you from assuming you know how best to serve them when they return. Asking about their needs also shows them that you care and are eager to help. They may not know what they need at first, but as time gets closer, they likely will have a list. Try to fulfill as much of it as possible, and be honest about what you can't. The worst thing you can do is overpromise and underdeliver!

As you plan, consider some of the following questions:

> » Who will greet the missionaries at the airport? (After long flights, they may not want this.)
> » What will their housing needs be?
> » What will their transportation needs be?
> » Will they need additional financial support?
> » Can the church stock their pantry so they don't have to go immediately to the grocery store?
> » What are the church's expectations for them while they are back? Have you communicated these expectations?
> » What are their expectations of the church while they are back? Have you asked?
> » How can the church love their children well?
> » How can the church assist them with debriefing and (if needed) counseling?
> » How will the church allow them to report?
> » How might they become active in the church's local mission again (if desired)?

For more details to help you plan well, the Appendix can direct you to a "Returning Missionaries Checklist."

Presence

If you do nothing else as a church for your returning missionaries, be relationally present. Try to be sensitive to how much they need space and how much they need community. It's going to be different for each missionary. They will likely want and need some time to rest and settle in, so don't plan any events in the beginning (unless requested). If they go quiet, simply check in occasionally. When the time is right, ask good questions and really listen. You may need to train some church members in how to do this. Fitting questions include:

» How are you doing today? (Each day has its unique ups and downs.)
» What's something that excites you about your time here?
» What's hard about being back here?
» What were some of the special moments of this past term?
» What was hard about this past term?
» How do you feel like you've changed since you first left?
» What do you love most about where you served?
» Can you tell me about some of the people you worked with?

Thoughtful questions like these begin to open the door for debriefing. Debriefing simply means talking through an experience after it has taken place. It is essential to the health of returning missionaries to experience debriefing each time they return. Any church can provide some basic measure of debriefing. For example, you might give each missionary a copy of Melissa Chaplin's workbook *Returning Well: Your Guide to Thriving Back "Home" After Serving Cross-Culturally* or Shonna Ingram's *Your Re-entry Path: Help for the Transition Season*. Then, as they make their way through the workbook, you can offer to meet occasionally to process their reflections.

Another example of debriefing comes from a sending church that utilizes what they call "The Heart Debrief." This debrief includes four simple questions:

» What are treasures to be celebrated?
» What are wounds to be healed?
» What are losses to be grieved?
» What are changes to be acknowledged?

The questions are given in advance for reflection, and then the

RECEIVING MISSIONARIES DURING REENTRY

missionaries have as long as they want to share. The church representative(s) (whether pastor, advocate, or friend) then listens actively and empathetically, not seeking to resolve anything, but only to bear witness to the missionaries' experiences. This can be a powerful use of your presence.

Keep in mind that there are limitations around debriefing. For instance, some missionaries may not feel comfortable answering such deep, personal questions. They might fear what you would think of their honest responses. Furthermore, many churches cannot provide professional debriefing and counseling. Especially in situations of trauma, it may be best to utilize a professional third party for debriefing and counseling. Some churches offer to pay for a set number of these services during each return, which can richly supplement the care the church provides. In order to explore debriefing more deeply, the Appendix can direct you to the resource "Re-Entry Guide for Those Returning for Good."

Provision

Finally, provide all that you have committed to provide. One of the best ways to facilitate this is by writing a "reentry plan." Take what you have gleaned from the early stages of your planning and presence, and work with the missionary to write this plan. This plan will give an overview of the steps needed to make the return as healthy as possible. To keep it from being overwhelming, try to make it no more than one page.

The Reentry Plan

There are a number of ways you can organize a reentry plan. It can simply be a checklist, but it may be helpful to provide categories to show the range of care provided (and to keep you from forgetting something important). You might also break the plan down according to each family member. One sending church uses the following categories: logistics, debriefing, reconnecting, reporting, and releasing. Below is an example of a reentry plan using those categories:

» Logistics «

+ The church will provide a rental car for up to three months.
+ The church will help search for affordable missionary housing.

» Debriefing «

+ For the couple: The church will provide at least one debriefing session with the missions pastor and two paid sessions with a counselor.
+ For the children: The church will provide at least one debriefing session with the children's pastor and two paid sessions with an art therapist.

» Reconnecting «

+ The missionaries will have at least one evening dinner with the lead pastor and family to refresh relationships.
+ The missionaries will prayer walk the church's neighborhood and recommend fresh ways for the church to engage, especially with internationals.

» Reporting «

+ The missionaries will have one 10-minute report in a Sunday worship service with a reception to follow and one 60-minute report at a missions event with a reception to follow.
+ The missionaries will join a small group and report

informally as part of group participation.

» Releasing «

+ The missionaries will be recommissioned at a Sunday worship service prior to departure.
+ The church will provide a farewell cookout with family, friends, and small group members.

There are a few things to keep in mind when finalizing the plan. First, be sure the missionaries get to shape it according to their needs and feel pleased with it. Remember that they will also have expectations to fulfill from their missions organization, extended family, and other supporting churches (those entities may already be providing for some of their needs as well). And finally, in light of the many demands on them plus their navigation of reverse culture shock, be flexible with the plan. Staying in regular communication with them allows you to do this well.

The Reentry Team

As you can see, receiving missionaries during reentry can be a demanding task. Putting the responsibility for it on one person—even a full-time staff member—can be too much. Reentry is the perfect opportunity to mobilize church members to help, as we discussed in Chapter 5, "Involving the Entire Church." In his book *The Reentry Team: Caring for Your Returning Missionaries*, Neal Pirolo recommends training a group of people responsible for different aspects of return care. If you have developed an advocate team (see Chapter 12, "Providing Ongoing Care"), they can serve in this way. A missions committee might also be an effective team.

You may be surprised to find that church members with no missions experience or interest get excited about reentry care. For example, a real estate agent might enjoy finding housing for returning missionaries. Or there may be a family with an extra vehicle they can loan freely. Who in your church loves to start meal trains? Let them organize one and also be in charge of filling the missionaries' pantry. Is there an empty-nest couple in the church who loves to spend time with children? Ask them to provide occasional childcare while the parents take date nights. Do you have up-and-coming missionary candidates? Let them be on the frontlines of carrying out reentry care. This will be beneficial for everyone involved. And of course, invite the wisdom and participation of any former missionaries in your church as well.

The Safe Harbor

Imagine the moment Jesus returned to heaven after his missionary journey. What an honorable welcome he must have received! As he sat down at the right hand of his Father, he was surely showered with love and safe from any further harm. In a similar way, when our missionaries return from their mission, whether it's for a short time or permanently, we do well to honor them and provide a safe harbor for them. This is pleasing to our Father.

Walking through reentry can be a disorienting experience. Like Paul Bäumer's return from World War I, a veil will inevitably lie between the returnees and their culture of origin. The sending church that receives them may have no personal experience of reentry with which to relate, but they can, by the power of the Holy Spirit, empathize and learn. They can "rejoice with those who rejoice, [and] weep with those who weep" (Romans 12:15). Through planning, presence, and provision, returning missionaries can feel truly loved and known. They can set sail again in obedience to the sending God through the love and care of his sending church.

SENDING CHURCH ELEMENT #16:
INNOVATING AS SENDING CHURCHES

By Nathan Sloan

"

A sending church innovates by honestly reevaluating itself according to the Sending Church Elements, while also researching new missions trends and practices. This practice provides the opportunity to assess its entire approach. Based on this assessment, church leaders then make necessary changes and communicate those changes to church members and missionaries.

Thomas Edison is commonly credited as the inventor of the incandescent light bulb, one of the greatest inventions in modern history. What is often overlooked, however, is that more than forty years before commercializing his revolutionary product, inventors were already demonstrating that constant electric light was possible, and they were working on a lamp and filament that could sustain the light. Edison and his team then came along and fashioned a carbon filament that could last up to twelve hundred hours. When it became the standard for electrical lighting around the world—changing forever how we harness and use energy—the fame of Edison's accomplishment led us to forget one thing: his work was more innovation than invention.

The Necessity of Change

Innovation can be defined simply as introducing something new about an existing product or practice. We experience innovation all the time with each release of a new phone, new car model, and even those pesky software updates. Of course, the "early adopter" crowd tends to welcome such changes eagerly. But many of us are hesitant about change at first. Sometimes we are outright obstinate, such as in the case of big changes, like political shifts in our country, or small changes, like new road construction. We get used to the way things are. Change threatens us.

This has often been the case in local churches. We grow accustomed to how a pastor preaches, how the music is played, and how the programs are structured. Familiarity is a comfort to us. So, when innovation is introduced, it inevitably shakes the foundation, sometimes even resulting in arguments, divisions, and departures. Thus, some churches prefer to continue headstrong in the same patterns, even if it means they slowly lose touch with their community and mission.

But change can be a good thing, and in an industrialized, globalized, technological world, it is actually a necessary thing. Throughout this book, we have encouraged you to build the culture, vision, strategy, and practices of a sending church. Applying those first fifteen elements will take a lot of work, but once you are developing, sending, and receiving back missionaries, it will likely feel as though the engine is humming along and simply needs to be maintained. Merely aiming for maintenance, however, would be a mistake. It is often when you think things are just the way they should be that innovation is needed. The world is not the same as when you started your sending journey!

The Amish of Global Missions

Several years ago, my co-author Bradley Bell wrote an article titled "The Danger of Focusing Only on Unreached People Groups" (UPG).[1] The UPG framework has shaped missions strategy since Ralph Winter popularized it in 1974 at the Lausanne Congress for World Evangelization. The article was not written to dismiss this important missions strategy; instead, it was a nod toward innovation. Bradley acknowledged complex changes in the world, such as migration and urbanization, that blurred the lines of former people group boundaries. Some people groups could still be engaged as mono-cultural, mono-lingual units in a single geographical area. But others, many in fact, were in the process of merging or emerging as part of a global stew. In light of such dynamics, the article suggested, it could be ineffective to make reaching UPGs our only missions strategy.

As you might imagine, the suggestion did not receive a warm welcome by everyone. The president of one large missions organization even responded publicly with his thoughts, and they were not happy ones. It became a lesson for us as we sought to push such conversations "upstream," beyond missiological mainstream thought and practice. The UPG strategy was tightly bound to a moment in history. Any innovation felt threatening.

Consider this analogy. If you travel through Pennsylvania today, you will likely encounter some part of the Amish community. The Amish are a group of Swiss-German origin who maintain mostly the same lifestyle that they did when they arrived in North America in the eighteenth century. They have rejected most conveniences of modern technology, choosing horse and buggy over motor vehicles, mule and plow over farm machinery and one-room schoolhouses over the modern education system. The Amish have a rich way of life, but one mostly out of touch with the rest of the world.

Similarly, without innovation in a rapidly changing world, our churches could become the Amish of global missions. Would remaining out of touch with a changing world help us accomplish God's mission? Furthermore, has our era of missions history captured the perfect way to obey the Great Commission? These are essential questions for a sending church to consider, and it could make all the difference for a global stew of lost people.

The Student of Global Trends

As a sending church leader, how can you embrace change and innovation in missions instead of rage against it? One way is by being a curious student of global trends. Picture yourself in the year 1990. The internet is still up and coming. International travel is still pre-9/11. No one on the planet has a smartphone. Now, ask yourself, how has the world changed in the last thirty years? How has this change impacted global missions engagement? In many ways it feels like we live on a different planet.

Now consider what will change in the *next* thirty years. What is already happening that will change the world and our missions engagement in it? We're not talking about having to predict the future—we're talking about living on your tiptoes leaning forward rather than on your heels pushing back. For example, how might artificial intelligence (AI) provide opportunities to spread the gospel rather than just being a threat to our current way of life? Have you learned how to use it (or at least become aware of how it's already part of your life)? When some "upstream" thinker suggests a way to use AI in our missions engagement, will you be ready to consider it, or will it cause some unhappy thoughts?

Nineteenth-century missionary Hudson Taylor was ready for innovation when he encountered the limitations of "coastal missions"—that is, the strategy of preaching the gospel on coastlands as the means of reaching people. Instead, he established the precedent of "inland missions," intentionally pressing into the interior of a nation with the gospel. He also adopted the clothing and customs of the indigenous people he served. These were forward-thinking missiological strategies that changed the way missionaries engaged large geographical areas.

No doubt Taylor was a student of global trends and the shifts happening in the world around him. How much more can you be such a student? You've got resources and technology that far exceed what Hudson Taylor had available to him. Stay in touch with world news, be a student of the global church, and keep an eye out for books on shifts in missions. It will impact how your sending church moves forward.

The Honest Evaluator

Another way to embrace change is by regularly and honestly reevaluating yourself according to the Sending Church Elements. We see this happening in healthy sending churches all the time. A leader (often alongside his or her team or committee) looks back at the elements and considers places of weakness (or at least practices that can be made even better). This evaluation is made even more effective (albeit possibly more humbling) by inviting your missionaries into the evaluation process. They certainly have a helpful perspective to share with your church.

For example, one sending church did this evaluation and realized they had narrowed their definition of a missionary to only those who do it as a full-time vocation. That meant their sending pipeline was structured only for a specific type of person. Meanwhile, their church was full of professionals who could take their jobs overseas. So, they decided to innovate their vision and strategy (see Chapters 3 and 4) and expanded their identification, assessment, and development processes (see Chapters 7–9) to include professionals, retirees, those studying abroad, and more. And they just recently commissioned their very first marketplace missionary.

Of course, it might feel overwhelming to consider a complete overhaul of how you send. But that's not the suggestion here. Think of it more like a rock-climbing rope. Only a fool would ascend a rock face with a cotton rope from the local department store. Or imagine him descending with a bungee cord. The cotton rope would be inflexible, and the bungee cord would be too flexible. Instead, a rock climbing rope is made with material that allows it to flex without breaking or overstretching. That's the nature of an innovative sending church. It is dynamic rather than static. It has a firm structure but can change and adapt as needed.

Just think, this process might even lead you to discover a new sending church element or a form of missions engagement that moves beyond the sending paradigm. That's right, we recognize that sending as we have described it here will always need innovation, and that's okay. In fact, that's why we dedicated the book, in part, "to the churches that will make [the elements] better." Change can be hard, but innovation leads toward greater health and deeper maturity.

To help you with this, we've listed two resources in the Appendix: "Personal Evaluation & Reflection as a Missions Leader" and "Sending Church Assessment." Both of these can be utilized on your own, or Upstream leaders would be glad to assist you as part of our consulting ministry.

Communicating Change

As a final word of wisdom on innovation, when you do decide to make these exciting changes, remember to communicate them well to your church and missionaries. In some cases, it may be best to familiarize them with the idea long before it goes into implementation. Be patient with their hesitations and gracious with their criticisms. Assure them of your commitment to what will never change: the gospel, the Great Commission, and your love for them. They'll come around.

Or they might not. I know one lay missions pastor who put great effort into expanding his church's missions convictions (see Chapter 2), but when he rolled them out, they were rejected by the staff, missionaries, and congregation. The church had not been introduced to the concept of missions convictions and liked their unwritten ways of doing things. The innovation clearly wasn't going to happen, at least not for a while. It was discouraging, but it also gave him a new prayer for his church: that God would prepare people's hearts to embrace the change in his perfect timing. Dependence on God for needed change is always a good thing.

Christ's Lampstands

One of the things I love about my city, Louisville, Kentucky, is that just a few years after Thomas Edison's innovation became available, Louisville played host to the largest display of incandescent light bulbs in the world. At an annual world fair called the Southern Exposition, forty-five acres in the heart of the city were lit by 5,000 bulbs. That might not have been impressive to us whose eyes are accustomed to entire metropolises beaming in the night sky, but in that day, it was the largest display of incandescent lights the world had ever seen. My humble city displayed what can happen when dreamers, thinkers, and innovators push new ideas until they are finally realized.

Local churches are called to shine as Christ's lampstands (see Revelation 1:20). His presence within them beams in the darkness. Let us not resist displaying and communicating his gospel to an ever-changing world. Instead, let's send out heralds of that gospel light to the ends of the earth and do so with all the innovation required for such a task. This is how sending churches shine the brightest.

SENDING CHURCH ELEMENT #17: INFLUENCING OTHER CHURCHES

By Nathan Sloan

> **"**
>
> *A sending church influences other churches when it pursues relationships with like-minded and/or neighboring churches who haven't matured as far in sending. The church thus multiplies its sending capacity by sharing experiences and resources with other churches, possibly even leading to strategic partnerships.*

I finished my curry, picked up my cup of chai, and continued to listen to the missions leaders around me. For the last couple years, eight of us had gathered monthly for Indian food, friendship, and a place to help one another as we faced challenges in our ministries. Over time this small band of men and women had become a real gift to me in the highs and lows of leading missions in my local church.

Go back two years, and the picture was very different. I was fairly isolated as a missions leader. Sure, I knew a few mission pastors in the area and had a decent network of missions colleagues around the country. But close relationships were really lacking.

One day, I was having lunch with one of the missions pastors in my city, and we were lamenting that we didn't connect more. He and I knew of six or eight other missions leaders nearby, but we didn't know them well. We realized that if we could rally them together, we would all benefit greatly. So, over the next few months, through emails, texts, and phone calls, we started a small, informal missions pastor network in Louisville, Kentucky. It was nothing fancy, but it was meaningful.

Our little group lasted about five years. During that time, some left, others joined, and then we ultimately disbanded. But while it lasted, it was a blessing, a wonderful community of leaders who grew to trust one another and freely shared ideas and resources. Each of our ministries matured because of our influence on one another. To this day, I believe it was one of the most formative parts of my time as a missions pastor.

Building Relationships

I hope you see the central factor in this exchange of wisdom and influence: relationships. Often, we think of influence in terms of notoriety—platforming ourselves and gaining followers. We assume that if people know how successful we are, they will seek our expertise. And though that might well lead to having influence through things like books and conferences, the most lasting impact almost always comes through relationships.

We were built for relationships. This is true in life and in missions. Relationships are how influence spreads in the sending church world. I love that you're reading this Upstream book, but you need to know that any expertise we have has come from a collective of missions leaders and churches around the world. In a sense, we are sending church "curators." These leaders have been generous, but they've also been friends. It's relationships that lead people to share.

These relationships are built on trust. We're all familiar with how churches in our town end up with a stereotype or two. "Oh, that's the First Christian Church, and the way they do missions is different." But sit down with their missions leader, and you might be surprised at how much you have in common. Meet up again, and you may discover you have some things to learn from each other. Start connecting once a month, and you'll probably find yourself a little more encouraged, maybe even a little less lonely.

It's this kind of community that often leads to collaboration. It can be as simple as a phone call asking, "Could I get your insight on this?"—after which you end up with a bit of wisdom that is exactly what you needed. Or, if neither of you have experience in the matter, perhaps you'll work together to create something new. We've even heard of church leaders who decide to partner together in their ministries. For instance, three sending churches in the same town decided to band together to fully fund a missionary from one of their churches. How did that come about? Furthermore, how was it accomplished without confusion or conflict? Through trusting, collaborative relationships built over time.

If you'd like to take steps toward developing your own band of missions leaders (whether locally, domestically, or globally), see the Appendix's "How to Build Relationships with Other Local Church Missions Leaders."

Building the Kingdom

If you are actively applying the Sending Church Elements and on your way to sending one missionary from your church, you are likely way ahead of most churches' missions engagement. There are many faithful churches we would describe as "supporting churches"—that is, churches that support missions efforts through finances, prayer, and some level of relationship, but that outsource all the rest to missions organizations. As a sending church leader, you can certainly learn and benefit from relationships with supporting church leaders. However, your potential to influence *them* is massive.

If you trace back the story of most sending churches, you will usually find there was a catalyst for growing beyond just being a supporting church. I had the privilege of being that catalyst at my church. I was a returned missionary who was captivated by the church at Antioch in Acts 11–18. I wanted to experience a modern-day Antioch in my own Christian journey, so I helped build a sending culture. Along the way, God provided other sending church leaders who answered my emails, sat with me over coffee, and picked up the phone when I needed wisdom and a listening ear. They helped me catalyze sending in a way that continues today, even though I am no longer the church's missions pastor.

Just think, you could be that kind of catalyst—not just at one church, but at many churches. You could be the one captivated by the Bible's sending vision who then takes time to build relationships with other church leaders and helps them imagine more than supporting. Pouring your life into a single sending church will no doubt bring kingdom impact, but consider the exponential impact of multiplying sending churches. What a tremendous way to build the kingdom. That's exactly what this last sending church element is all about.

Here's another way to think about it. As your church is ministering to the nations through the missionaries you've sent, you are helping those new disciples and churches become recipients of the gospel. But you don't just want them to be *recipients*; you want them to grow and mature to the point that they become *senders* as well. What a joy to take what you've learned as a sending church and help other parts of the global church embrace and contextualize it.

Recently, Upstream had a sending church reach out to us with this kind of kingdom vision. They had so benefited from the precursor to this book, *The Sending Church Defined*, that they wanted to fund its translation into Spanish so that their colleagues in Spanish-speaking churches could access and implement it as well. That church is doing fantastic work within its own sending practices, and now they are being catalysts for sending around the world. In other words, they are influencing other churches.

Another way that some churches are spreading their influence is by investing back into Upstream. They do this by sharing their best practices, participating in the leadership of cohorts and training, writing for the Upstream blog, hosting and inviting churches to regional Upstream events, communicating Upstream's impact by word of mouth, funding strategic projects, and becoming financial supporters. We call these friends "E17 churches"—because they are carrying out Element #17. They are advancing the sending church movement by extending Upstream's reach to new churches around the world. For more information on this, see "Partnering with Upstream to Influence Other Churches" as directed in the Appendix.

Being Built up Ourselves

Influence is not simply a one-way street, however. When we seek out reciprocal relationships, take the posture of learners, and become generous with what we've learned, we are changed. Any missionary can testify to this principle. As they pour their lives into the people of another culture, they often find themselves filled up as they fall in love with the culture and the people. In time, the foreign culture may even begin to feel like their own culture and family. Sure, they've influenced others. But in the process, they've been influenced in ways they never imagined.

As the global church continues to grow in remarkable ways, the Western part of the global church has a great opportunity to be built up by our brothers and sisters of other nations. For example, the Western church has learned to send people in ways that typically require a tremendous amount of money. In developing countries, however, the church is sending in ways that still depend on generosity, but not on extensive wealth. We could stand to learn a thing or two from them about expanding our sending to

SENDING CHURCH ELEMENT #17

more than a middle-class phenomenon.

Also, in light of globalization, the global church is naturally more multiethnic, which is being reflected in their sending. Picture an international church in Kenya sending a Chinese family who is taking a job building highways in the Middle East. This may seem bizarre, but it's actually more reflective of the diversity we see in the church at Antioch (Acts 11–13). And it's a rich foretaste of the new heavens and earth, which will play host to "the glory and the honor of the nations" (Revelation 21:26). What a privilege for Western churches to be influenced in this regard, pushing past racial and ethnic boundaries to send with unity in diversity.

Friends around the Table

Sending Church Element #17 is probably the most neglected aspect of the entire framework, largely because it comes in at the very last, and churches are busy with the work of the first sixteen elements. But this is a tragic reality. We have a wonderful opportunity before us to build relationships, build the kingdom, and be built up ourselves.

As a final motivator, remember that Indian curry and chai that awaits you among friends and colleagues. This is a small picture of the sending God gathering his people around his table at the marriage supper of the Lamb, men and women who have been saved and given purpose and passion for the nations. I experienced it for those five years, and it helped shape the way I see and engage in ministry. Imagine what it could mean for you. So, why wait? Send an email, shoot some text messages, or call a few missions leader friends, and start making space for these kinds of relationships.

CONCLUSION

The greatest discoveries don't just happen overnight.

Take, for instance, the periodic table. In 1789 French chemist Antoine Lavoisier was the first to begin arranging the elements into a table divided by metals and non-metals. Then in 1829 German chemist Johann Wolfang Döbereiner further ordered the table by elements with similar properties. In 1860 at the first international conference of chemistry in Karlsruhe, Germany, the elements were positioned as we know them today, by their atomic masses. Soon after, British chemist John Newlands altered the periodic table by the known elements, followed by Russian chemist Dmitri Mendeleev, who created gaps for undiscovered elements.[1]

That was a lot of hard words to pronounce. But what this means is the understanding of the elements as an orderly periodic table was a progressive, collaborative, and global process. It was built on centuries of study, each successive generation dependent on the other. And beyond the banner of one nationality, it now serves a worldwide community as a product of a worldwide community. Wow!

If we may, the Sending Church Elements are not so dissimilar. With the Bible as the foundation, along with centuries of missions history, and the contributions of sending churches around the world, this "table of elements" was arranged. It is not the product of one person, nor even of the four authors of this book. Instead, it draws on the collective wisdom of faithful church leaders, missionaries, and missiologists. And if it is to stand the test of time, it will need future generations to build upon it.

Will you put it into practice?

We hope you will! And we hope you'll share what you learn. You see, Upstream isn't just a missions organization. It's more of a movement, a witness to what God is doing in his church. Missions has rolled downstream in the same ways for too long, leaving local churches on the shores. Join us in pressing "upstream," against the current, to the source from which missions is meant to flow: the sending God and his sending church. These seventeen elements will show you how to do that. They are more than the sending church *defined*. They are the sending church *applied*.

As you go, we'd like to recommend a few ways to be further equipped.

Resources

It was tempting for us to include an Appendix that was bigger than the book itself. That's because we have dozens of practical resources for everything we've talked about in these pages. These are guides, often adapted from churches, that can be plugged directly into your ministry. You can access many of them for free at theupstreamcollective.org/resources. Better yet, we encourage you to become an Upstream member, which gives you access not only to all our resources, but to everything we release in the future. You can do that at theupstreamcollective.org/join.

Cohorts

The most common Upstream service that missions leaders rave about is our cohorts.Our books are helping church leaders all around the world, but books are far better when applied in the context of community. Although we offer a variety of cohorts, our most popular (and the most relevant to this book) is our Sending Church Elements cohort. Imagine learning alongside fellow leaders about one element at a time, while also receiving one-on-one coaching in between group calls. We've heard people say it's the best thing they've ever done for their ministry. How can you argue with that? Find out more at theupstreamcollective.org/cohorts.

Training and Consulting

Sometimes leaders just need something specific. We often get requests from churches, missions organizations, and missionaries to provide customized help. And that's what our team is here for! Whether it's training on a particular topic at your church, partnering to create content for your organization, or simply receiving some consultation and encouragement from an Upstream leader, please reach out to us. Or if you've come up with something really great (like a new element) and you just want to share it with others, let us know. You can contact us anytime at info@theupstreamcollective.org.

Upstream Sending

Finally, after years of equipping sending churches we began receiving a common request: senders were looking for a missions organization that gives local churches a meaningful role in sending and sustaining their missionaries. In response we expanded our ministry to include a church-centric global sending organization called Upstream Sending. This means we not only equip churches to send well in partnership with any missions organization, but we also provide—for those who so choose—the structure, services, and relationships that allow churches to take the lead in sending their own people cross-culturally. For more information, we invite you to visit upstreamsending.com, or better yet, start a conversation with us at contact@upstreamsending.com.

A Sending Benediction

Well, we began this book with a sending church blessing. And if you've reached this point, then we hope that you *have been* blessed. Well done for sticking with it! You get an A+ in sending church chemistry.

Now all that's left is to pray for you as you explore, experiment with, and apply the elements for yourself.

Father, we thank you for this dear reader. We pray that he or she will not be overwhelmed with the content of these pages, but instead be compelled by the beauty of who you are as our great sending God. Guide this reader by your Spirit one step at a time. Use this reader in his or her sent identity, sent to bless the nations through the church. Thank you for allowing this reader—and us—to be part of your big, collaborative, global work. What a privilege! Come soon, Lord Jesus, we pray. And until you do, help us be faithful and fruitful in your mission. Amen.

APPENDIX: RESOURCES ON OUR WEBSITE

Instead of a massive Appendix, we have identified our best resources for each Sending Church Element, which are available for download on the Upstream website. Simply visit theupstream-collective.org and type the name of the resource listed below into the search box at the top of the page.

For all of our articles, resources, trainings, and cohorts organized according to each Sending Church Element, visit theupstream-collective.org/resources, scroll to the Sending Church Elements graphic, and click on whichever element you'd like to explore. Most of them are available for free, and all of them are available to Upstream members (you can become a member at theupstream-collective.org/join).

Element #1: Cultivating Missions Awareness
>> Cultivating Missions Awareness Ideas
>> Cultivating Missions Awareness Worksheet
>> Redeeming Short-term Trips

Element #2: Establishing Missions Convictions
>> Establishing Missions Convictions Worksheet
>> Examples of Missions Convictions

Element #3: Developing a Vision
>> Developing a Vision Examples
>> Developing a Vision Worksheet

Element #4: Building a Strategy
>> Focus & Funding Model Development Explained
>> Budgeting Template

Element #5: Involving the Entire Church
>> Developing a Sending Pipeline

» Missions Leadership Team Development
» Developing an International Ministry

Element #6: Evaluating Sending Pathways & Partners
» Questions for Evaluating Missions Organizations
» Questions for Evaluating On-Field Partners

Element #7: Identifying Missionaries
» Proactively Identifying Missionaries
» Walking through Calling with a Potential Missionary

Element #8: Assessing Missionaries
» Characteristics of Qualified Missionaries
» Health Assessment & Church Interview Guide

Element #9: Developing Missionaries
» Writing a Personal Development Plan
» Personal Development Plan Template

Element #10: Commissioning Missionaries
» Commissioning Examples
» Sending Commitment Template

Element #11: Getting Missionaries Established
» Learning Missionary Skills (IPOC3)
» 90-Day On-Ramping Checklist for Newly Launched Missionaries

Element #12: Providing Ongoing Care
» Establishing Advocacy Teams
» Missionary Health Diagnostic

Element #13: Maintaining Strategic Focus
» Strategic Reflection Questions Missionaries Should Ask
» Simple Annual Review of a Missionary from a Sending

Church Template

Element #14: Inviting Missionaries' Influence
- » Influencing Your Sending Church
- » Inviting a Missionary's Influence in Your Church

Element #15: Receiving Missionaries during Reentry
- » Returning Missionaries Checklist
- » Re-Entry Guide for Those Returning for Good

Element #16: Innovating as Sending Churches
- » Personal Evaluation & Reflection as a Missions Leader
- » Sending Church Assessment

Element #17: Influencing Other Churches
- » How to Build Relationships with Other Local Church Missions Leaders
- » Partnering with Upstream to Influence Other Churches

ACKNOWLEDGEMENTS

Bradley: When I think of the Sending Church Elements, I think of driving through the Blue Ridge Mountains at night. At least I think that's where we were—I was in the backseat capturing our notes. Larry McCrary had come up with his latest idea—these "parts" of a sending church—and he wanted input from Nathan and me. It was a classic Upstream moment: friends sharing long missiological conversations, agreeing, disagreeing, laughing, and, ultimately, discovering something meaningful—the Sending Church Elements. I am grateful for that car ride (and that I don't get car sick). I'm also grateful for how Mike Easton stepped into the project with the full force of an Iowa wind storm. If he did not contribute his own expertise and pull together the thoughts of four scattered authors, we may never have published this thing. Thanks also to the fantastic Upstream Publishing team who works with such excellence because they're awesome, but also because they believe in the mission: Jodie Sigrest, Hayley Moss, David McWhite, Jamie Chaplin, and Meredith Cook. Well done, my friends!

Mike: Thanks to Cornerstone Church for being my sending church and giving me the opportunity to lead the church's missions vision for many years. My understanding of being a pastor and a leader in global missions is due to the investment of many in my life through the church. Thanks to all who chose to go from Cornerstone to the nations. Your bravery and passion for the gospel will forever be an example to me. Thanks to Upstream for the opportunity to learn what it means to be a sending church and to lead other churches towards that through equipping and writing. Thanks to Reliant for being a great sending partner for Cornerstone's missionaries and now giving me the opportunity to provide leadership in our ministry. Thanks to my parents, who let me get that English degree from Iowa State University. It finally paid off! Thanks to my lovely wife, Emily, who has kept my confidence up over many years of marriage. And thanks to my kids, Nora, Brooks, Beck, and Jax, for bringing great joy into my life. I pray that God would use you to bring the gospel to the nations.

Larry: Well, I would be remiss if I did not also mention the infamous car ride, but, honestly, so much of what I have learned about the sending church really is an observation of how Brad, Mike, and Nathan have worked out these ideas in the local church for many years. They are missiologically deep and also great practitioners, and they have been a true inspiration for me. I am also grateful for the hundreds of churches that we have worked with over the years around the world that are living out these Sending Church Elements, churches of different sizes and backgrounds all committed to carrying out the role they have in the Great Commission.

Nathan: I, too, remember the car ride Brad mentioned in his acknowledgment. We crafted something meaningful that day. But it's just a picture of my friendship with Larry and Brad. Over the last fifteen years these two men have been some of my best friends and closest colleagues. We have wrestled through rich missological issues, sat and lamented in seasons of suffering, and laughed during moments of joy. This book is the fruition of so many of these conversations and experiences. Thank you men for living life with me and for locking arms to help churches send well. I also want to thank my church, Sojourn Church Midtown, for allowing me to serve as their missions pastor. My writing in this book is the overflow of my ministry within the body of Sojourn.

ENDNOTES

Sending Church Element #1

1 Caleb Crider, *Tradecraft: For the Church on Mission* (Urban Loft Publishers: Portland, 2013), 22–23.

Sending Church Element #2

1 Caleb Crider, Larry McCrary, Rodney Calfee, and Wade Stephens, *Tradecraft: For the Church on Mission* (Urban Loft Publishers: Portland, 2013), 35.

2 John Piper and Tom Stellar, "Driving Convictions Behind Foreign Missions at Bethlehem: Bethlehem's Commitment to Missions," Desiring God, January 1, 1996, https://www.desiringgod.org/articles/driving-convictions-behind-foreign-missions.

3 Jayson Georges, *The 3D Gospel: Ministry in Guilt, Shame, and Fear Cultures* (Timē Press, 2014), 10-12.

Sending Church Element #3

1 John F. Kennedy Presidential Library and Museum, "Address to Joint Session of Congress May 15, 1961," educational video, 8:01, https://www.jfklibrary.org/learn/about-jfk/historic-speeches/address-to-joint-session-of-congress-may-25-1961#:~:text=While%20listing%20national%20goals%2C%20the,.%22%20This%20excerpt%20ends%20abruptly.

2 "Can You Share Your Life Story in Exactly Six Words?" NPR, February 3, 2010, https://www.npr.org/templates/story/story.php?storyId=123289019.

Sending Church Element #4

1 Alek Arend, "Nikola Jokic Gave the Classiest Answer When Asked If He's the Nuggets' Best Player," Athlon Sports, May 31, 2023, https://athlonsports.com/nba/nikola-jokic-classy-answer-nuggets-best-player.

2 David Horner, *When Missions Shapes the Mission: You and Your Church Can Reach the World* (Nashville: B&H Publishing Group, 2011), 169–70.

3 J.D. Greear, *Gaining By Losing: Why the Future Belongs to Churches That Send* (Grand Rapids: Zondervan, 2016), 111.

Sending Church Element #5

1 Michael T. Cooper, *Ephesiology: A Study of the Ephesian Movement* (Littleton, CO: William Carey, 2020), xiii.

2 Ellen Livingood, "What's Your Missions Pastor Profile?" Postings: The Missions Mobilizers' E-newsletter, Catalyst Services, vol. 11 issue 5 (May 2016), https://catalystservices.org/wp-content/uploads/2018/02/Whats-Your-Missions-Pastor-Profile.pdf.

3 Neal Pirolo, *Serving as Senders Today* (San Diego: Emmaus Road International, 2012).

4 Bradley Bell, *The Sending Church Defined*, 2nd ed. (Knoxville: Upstream, 2021).

5 R. Kent Hughes, *Acts: The Church Afire* (Wheaton, IL: Crossway, 1996), 255.

Sending Church Element #6

1 Ellen Livingood, "Choose Your National Church Partner Wisely," The Upstream Collective, October 31, 2022, https://www.theupstreamcollective.org/post/choose-your-national-church-partner-wisely.

Sending Church Element #7

1 Adapted from Nathan Sloan, who used this at Sojourn Church in Louisville, Kentucky.

2 David Frazier, *Mission Smart: 15 Critical Questions to Ask before Launching Overseas* (Memphis, TN: CreateSpace Independent Publishing Platform, 2013), 20.

3 Tim Keller, "Vocation: Discern Your Calling," 2011, http://storage.cloversites.com/highpeakfellowship/documents/Vocation-Discerning_Your_Calling.pdf.

Sending Church Element #8

1 Edward Judson, *Adoniram Judson, D. D., His Life and Labours* (London: Hodder & Stoughton, 1883), 577–78.

2 George W. Peters, *A Biblical Theology of Missions* (Chicago: Moody, 1984), 229.

3 The creation of the "Characteristics of an Effective Missionary" was heavily influenced by the teaching and personal mentorship of Nate Irwin, missions pastor at College Park Church in Indianapolis. Figure 2, "The Characteristics of an Ideal Missionary," has been adapted from a chapter I wrote in *Church on Mission:* Nathan Garth, "Pre-Field Missionary Assessment in the Context of the Local Church," in *Churches on Mission: God's Grace Abounding to the Nations*, eds. Geoffrey Hartt, Christopher Little, and John Wang, Evangelical Missiological Society Series, vol. 25 (Pasadena, CA: William Carey Library, 2017), 298–99.

4 Ryan Shaw, *Spiritual Equipping for Mission: Thriving as God's Message Bearers* (Downers Grove, IL: IVP Books, 2014), 34.

5 Although this section is written to married missionaries, single missionaries need to have strong relational connections as well. These can include deep friendships, close Christian community, or relationships with extended family that remains stateside.

6 Tom Steffen and Lois McKinney Douglas, *Encountering Missionary Life and Work: Preparing for Intercultural Ministry* (Grand Rapids, MI: Baker, 2008), 39.

7 Robert E. Speer, "What Essentially Constitutes a Missionary Call," in Turner, *The Call, Qualifications and Preparation of Candidates for Foreign Missionary Service* (Whitefish, MT: Kessinger, 2009), 6.

8 Ibid.

9 Bradley Bell, *The Sending Church Defined* (Knoxville: The Upstream Collective, 2015), 44.

10 Gerald E. Bates, "Who Is Qualified to Be Called as a Missionary?" Evangelical Missions Quarterly (October 1977), https://missionexus.org/who-is-qualified-to-be-called-as-a-missionary/.

11 Judith Anderson Koenig, *Assessing 21st Century Skills: Summary of a Workshop* (Washington, D.C.: National Academies Press, 2011), 63.

12 Andy Kampman, leader at Austin Stone Church (Austin, Texas) and

Launch Global. Email interview with the author, August 10, 2017.

13 Eric E. Wright, *A Practical Theology of Missions: Dispelling the Mystery, Recovering the Passion* (Ministry and Mission) (Leominster, UK: Day One, 2010), 188.

14 Evelyn Hibbert and Richard Hibbert, *Training Missionaries: Principles and Possibilities* (Pasadena, CA: William Carey Library, 2016), 39.

15 There are many noteworthy Bible and theology options available online including BibleMesh, Crosslands, and Ligonier Ministries. Also, at the time of writing, Reformed Theological Seminary and Dallas Theological Seminary, among others, offer a limited number of free online courses.

16 Perspectives is a well-known, and well-loved, fifteen-week global missions course hosted at regional sites. You can find out more on their website, www.perspectives.org.

17 *You Are Sent* is a nine-week global missions study. The course was created within a local church to help disciple members to see their sentness and grow in their passion for the nations. Nathan Sloan, *You Are Sent: Find Your Place in God's Global Mission* (Greensboro, NC: New Growth Press, 2022).

Sending Church Element #9

1 This list has been adapted from the author's writing in the book *Churches on Missions: God's Grace Abounding to the Nations* (Pasadena: William Carey Publishing, 2017).

2 This statement comes from the author's understanding of the five Great Commission passages: Matthew 28:18–20; Mark 16:15; Luke 24:47; John 20:21; Acts 1:8.

3 George W. Peters, *A Biblical Theology of Missions* (Chicago: Moody, 1984), 229.

4 Neal Pirolo, *Serving as Senders Today: How to Care for Your Missionaries as They Prepare to Go, Are on the Field and Return Home* (San Diego: Emmaus Road International, 2012), 56.

5 Thomas Hale and Gene Daniels, *On Being a Missionary,* rev. ed. (Pasadena, CA: William Carey Library, 2012), 54.

6 Harold R. Cook, *An Introduction to Christian Missions* (Chicago: Moody, 1974), 267.

7 A. Scott Moreau, Gary Corwin, and Gary B. McGee, *Introducing World Missions: A Biblical, Historical, and Practical Survey* (Grand Rapids: Baker, 2004), 170.

8 One of those organizations is our very own. The Upstream Collective is committed to helping every church see themselves as a sending church and every believer as a sent one. We have resources, cohorts, and coaching all geared toward sending churches and their leaders. If you want to go deep in any of these areas, check out our website, the-upstreamcollective.org, and let us know how we can help you.

9 The first pipeline comes from Sojourn Church Midtown in Louisville, Kentucky, and the second pipeline comes from Crosspointe Church in Columbus, Georgia.

Sending Church Element #12

1 For a more thorough biblical survey of missionary care than we can lay out in this chapter, plus step-by-step directions for application, see the Upstream book *Holding the Rope: How the Local Church Can Care for its Sent Ones* by Ryan Martin.

Sending Church Element #13

1 Andreas Illmer, "Mount Erebus disaster: The plane crash that changed New Zealand," BBC News, November 28, 2019, https://www.bbc.com/news/world-asia-50555046.

2 Peter Greer and Chris Horst, *Mission Drift: The Unspoken Crisis Facing Leaders, Charities, and Churches* (Grand Rapids: Bethany House Publishers, 2015).

3 See Tim Keller, "Leadership and Church Size Dynamics: How Strategy Changes with Growth," https://seniorpastorcentral.com/wp-content/uploads/2016/11/Tim-Keller-Size-Dynamics.pdf.

4 Ellen Livingood, "Annual Evaluations with Sent Ones: What They Should and Shouldn't Be," The Upstream Collective, December 15, 2022, https://www.theupstreamcollective.org/post/annual-evaluations-with-sent-ones-what-they-should-and- shouldn-t-be.

Sending Church Element #14

1 George W. Peters, *A Biblical Theology of Missions* (Chicago: Moody, 1984), 236.

Sending Church Element #15

1 Erich Maria Remarque, *All Quiet on the Western Front*, 1st ed. (Boston: Little, Brown, and Company, 1929), 246.

2 Kelly O'Donnell, *Missionary Care: Counting the Cost for World Evangelization* (Pasadena, CA: William Carey, 1999), 47.

3 Sarah Hay, et. al., *Worth Keeping* (Pasadena, CA: William Carey, 2013), 386.

4 O'Donnell, 310.

5 Marion Knell, *Burn Up or Splash Down: Surviving the Culture Shock of Re-entry* (Westmont, IL: IVP Books, 2007), 4.

6 Ibid., 226.

7 Hale and Daniels, 392.

Sending Church Element #16

1 Bradley Bell, "The Danger of Focusing Only on Unreached People Groups, Pt. 1," The Upstream Collective, September 19, 2022, https://www.theupstreamcollective.org/post/the-dangers-of-focusing-only-on-unreached-people-groups-part-one.

Conclusion

1 Deboleena M. Guharay, "A brief history of the periodic table," ASBMB Today, February 7, 2021, https://www.asbmb.org/asbmb-today/science/020721/a-brief-history-of-the-periodic-table#:~:text=In%201869%2C%20Russian%20chemist%20Dmitri,group%20he%20would%20rearrange%20them.

OTHER BOOKS FROM UPSTREAM COLLECTIVE

Tradecraft: For the Church on Mission

The Sending Church Defined

Listen: How to Make the Most of Your Short-Term Mission Trip

Holding the Rope: How the Local Church Can Care for Its Sent Ones

First 30 Daze: Practical Encouragement for Living Abroad Intentionally

The MarketSpace: Essential Relationships Between the Sending Church, Marketplace Worker, and Missionary Team

Receiving Sent Ones During Reentry: The Challenges of Returning "Home" and How Churches Can Help

Multisite Missions Leadership: The Challenges and Opportunities of Leading Missions at a Multisite Church

Lent and Missions: A 40-Day Devotional

The Missionary Mama's Survival Guide: Compassionate Help for the Mothers of Cross-Cultural Workers

Available on Amazon and theupstreamcollective.org

Made in the USA
Columbia, SC
22 November 2024

46603186R00150